*Leeah,
May your prayer life be filled with answers!
Bryant Buck*

The Prayer Warrior

By Bryant C. Buck

Copyright © 2007 by Bryant C. Buck

THE PRAYER WARRIOR
by Bryant C. Buck

Printed in the United States of America

ISBN 978-1-60266-535-4

All rights reserved solely by the author. The author guarantees all contents are original and do not infringe upon the legal rights of any other person or work. No part of this book may be reproduced in any form without the permission of the author. The views expressed in this book are not necessarily those of the publisher.

Unless otherwise indicated, Bible quotations are taken from the Authorized King James Version of the Bible, Copyright © 1975 by Thomas Nelson Inc., Publishers, Nashville, Tennessee.

www.xulonpress.com

Contents

INTRODUCTION vii
FOREWORD ix
SPLITTING THE TORNADO 15
HILLBILLY HEAVEN 19
A CHILD IN THE SHOW ME STATE 27
SUFFER THE LITTLE CHILDREN 31
PIGEONS AND HORSES 35
A DIFFICULT EDUCATION 39
SPRINGVALE 43
JOB STRUGGLES 49
AN ANGELIC PILLOW 53
HELEN OF STEWARTSVILLE 57
A CURVE IN THE ROAD 61
SEARCHING FOR THE TRUTH 65
A GROWING FAMILY 73
YAHWEH NISSI 79
THE JESUS MOVEMENT 85
NELSON KNITTING 91
THE DAY OF INFAMY 95
THE CREST OF THE WAVE 99
THE RIDOTT SHOP 103
THE FLORIDIAN 109
SAVING SALEM ACRES 113
PRAYER WARRING 117

SAWING OFF THE EIGHTIES	121
MOWING ALONG	125
ELDEN'S DAILY ROUTINE	129
THE MASTER CRAFTSMAN	133
THE END OF AN ERA	139
IT'S IN THE BOOK	145
PERSISTENCE PAYS OFF	149
NEW BEGINNINGS CHURCH	153
LIKE TWO PEAS IN A POD	157
WHERE TWO OR THREE	161
PASSING THE TORCH	167
ELDEN'S PRAYER PRINCIPLES	171
PRAYER PRINCIPLE ONE	171
PRAYER PRINCIPLE TWO	172
PRAYER PRINCIPLE THREE	173
PRAYER PRINCIPLE FOUR	174
PRAYER PRINCIPLE FIVE	175
PRAY WITHOUT CEASING	177
ACKNOWLEDGMENTS	181

INTRODUCTION

Usually biographies are written about famous people — presidents, generals, actors, etc. Elden Shisler is definitely none of the above. He isn't famous for anything; in fact, not very many people even know Elden. Yet Elden is definitely one of the most amazing people I have ever known in my life. Elden is amazing for one thing — his prayer life. I have never known anyone else in my life who has prayed so many fantastic prayers and then seen them come to pass.

If you sometimes wonder whether prayer really works or whether things you pray will ever come to pass, Elden's story should be an inspiration to you. If you question whether miracles still happen in this modern world, Elden's story should be an inspiration to you. And if you occasionally question how real the Almighty God can really be in your life, then the saga of Elden's life should truly be an inspiration to you.

Of course, you're probably wondering what great Bible college Elden attended or what great Christian leader he hung around with to become such a great man of prayer. The truth is that Elden never went to Bible college nor did he ever hang around with any great leaders of the Christian faith. Elden is a hillbilly from Missouri. He completed the 8th grade, but never finished high school. He was raised around people the world counts as nobodies. But when Elden Shisler prays, heaven moves!

THE PRAYER WARRIOR

Elden Shisler is a prayer warrior. In fact, to me he is THE PRAYER WARRIOR— hence the title of this book. Elden prays and prays and prays; when he is done praying, he prays some more. To put it another way, Elden is almost always praying no matter what else he is doing. And he never gives up! Just because God hasn't answered today doesn't mean that he won't answer tomorrow. Just because something is impossible today doesn't mean that God won't make it possible tomorrow. So Elden Shisler prays and never gives up. And heaven is moved to action by his prayers! This is the story of Elden Shisler — THE PRAYER WARRIOR. May his story be an inspiration to your prayer life as it has been to mine.

FOREWORD

The writing of this book presented a few problems. Three problems, in particular, presented themselves repeatedly. For your benefit as the reader, I will discuss these three problems briefly and how I dealt with each one in telling the story of Elden's life.

First, Elden Shisler is a Hebrew Christian. However, he has not always been a Hebrew Christian. Is there a problem with the fact that Elden is a Hebrew Christian? Not at all. Elden is very definitely a Christian first and a Hebrew Christian second. He has always put the emphasis in his life on a born-again experience with our Savior, faith, and prayer. These truths he shares with all other evangelical Christians. Nevertheless, Elden is a Hebrew Christian and as such has certain beliefs that he shares primarily just with other Hebrew Christians. One of these beliefs could not be avoided in recording the saga of Elden's life if I were to do justice to his life story.

Elden believes Christians should use the literal English transliterations of the original Hebrew names of the Almighty and His Son when referring to God and Jesus. Thus, where the vast majority of Christians refer to the heavenly Father as God, Elden refers to Him as Yahweh. Similarly, where the vast majority of Christians refer to the Son of our heavenly Father as Jesus, Elden refers to Him as Yahshua. But Elden did not reach the conclusion that he should use Yahweh and Yahshua in reference to the Almighty and His Son until he was 40 years old. Prior to that time, he said and wrote God and Jesus just like the great majority of English-speaking Christians do.

So how have I decided to handle this conviction of Elden's in writing this book? During the time in his life when Elden Shisler uses God and Jesus, I use God and Jesus. When he makes the transition to using Yahweh and Yahshua, I make the transition with him. So since Chapter One is a leap forward to a point in Elden's life after he has commenced using Yahweh and Yahshua, I use Yahweh and Yahshua in Chapter One. But then I go back to Elden's birth and record the saga of his life chronologically from that point to the present day. From Chapter 2 to Chapter 13 Elden is saying and writing God and Jesus in reference to the Almighty and His Son; so I use God and Jesus throughout these chapters. Then in Chapters 13 and 14 when Elden makes the transition to using Yahweh and Yahshua, I make the transition to using Yahweh and Yahshua with him. I primarily use Yahweh and Yahshua to refer to the Almighty and His Son throughout the remainder of Elden's life story.

Now someone is undoubtedly wondering why Elden uses Yahweh and Yahshua rather than God and Jesus. Since this book is primarily the story of Elden's amazing prayer life, at this point I will leave you wondering. In Chapter 14 when Elden makes his full transition to using Yahweh and Yahshua, I provide a brief explanation as to why he has this conviction.

Second, Elden Shisler has a number of miraculous experiences in his life. Since Elden is now 75 years of age, there is no one still alive with whom I could document the amazing experiences in his childhood. With these experiences I simply had to pick and choose. The truth is that I left a couple of his amazing childhood experiences out. The one miraculous experience from his childhood that I chose to include in the book is so close to a beloved story from the Bible that I felt I couldn't leave it out.

With the miraculous experiences in Elden's adult life, however, I attempted to document all of them with someone other than Elden himself. The miracle recorded in Chapter One and all the miraculous events in Elden's life recorded from Chapter Eight to the end of this book have been documented by someone other than Elden or one of his relatives. If you don't believe that the Almighty works miracles today, you will have a lot of explaining away to do when you read this book.

Finally, the majority of Elden's adult life is tied up in the life of his church Salem Temple Church (which it was called until just recently). Should I neglect the story of Elden's church? Should I tell the story of his church in great detail? Or should I tell the story of his church in part? Since many of Elden's prayers deal with the peace and prosperity of his church, I could not neglect the church's story entirely. On the other hand, since this is a book primarily about Elden's prayer life, neither could I tell the story of his church in great detail. So I decided to tell the story of Salem Temple Church in part. It is admitted right here that the story of Salem Temple Church is a sub-theme in this book.

But then the life and death struggles of a small country church provide a good sub-theme behind the major theme of Elden's amazing prayer life. Most of the books on the Christian market today are written by pastors and teachers with very successful Bible-believing churches. Often they are written by the leaders of the large mega-churches in metropolitan areas. However, a large number of Christians still attend smaller churches. If you attend a smaller church, it is my hope that you will identify to some degree with the struggles of Salem Temple Church.

THE PRAYER WARRIOR

With these brief explanations taken care of, I now proceed to a story that has been a tremendous inspiration to me — the saga of Elden Shisler's incredible prayer life. If you don't believe that prayer makes things happen, hopefully Elden's story will give you cause for reconsideration.

"PRAY WITHOUT CEASING"

I Thessalonians 5:17

CHAPTER ONE

SPLITTING THE TORNADO

Elden Shisler lives on a farm. In the 1970's this farm was known as Salem Acres, but since the early 1980's it has been called Lakeview Hills.

Lakeview Hills is situated in Stephenson County, Illinois about 14 miles northeast of the city of Freeport, Illinois and about 12 miles south of the Wisconsin state line. Although most of Illinois is flat, Stephenson County is an area of rolling hills in Northern Illinois. Lakeview Hills is located near the top of one of these rolling hills in the heart of Illinois' dairy land. Fields of corn and soybeans and hay dominate the area in fall and summer while snow generally covers the landscape the majority of each winter. Of course, herds of dairy cattle graze between the various fields just described. Lakeview Hills overlooks a small man-made lake on our neighbor's property just to the east of us — hence the name Lakeview Hills. A creek that generally flowed only in spring and early summer split the farm almost in half as it wound its way through a stand of trees. About halfway across the property from east to west and right on the edge of the stand of trees used to be a trash dump for nondisposable, nonperishable trash. And that brings us to this chapter's story.

THE PRAYER WARRIOR

First, I need to tell you about certain things that Elden consistently prays. Elden repeatedly prays that Yahweh (God) will control the weather on our behalf. In particular, he prays over and over that everyone who lives here will be protected from weather that might hazard our lives. You should know that Northern Illinois is in tornado country. We don't have hurricanes or earthquakes in this area, but rare is the year that we don't have at least one tornado or whirlwind which causes considerable damage. So, of course, Elden prays specifically that we will be protected from tornadoes. Moreover, he prays repeatedly that Yahweh will stop any tornado in its tracks if necessary to protect the residents of Lakeview Hills.

It was a hot afternoon in midsummer of 1982 when Elden hooked up the small wagon to the rider mower to haul some trash out to the dumping ground in front of the stand of trees. Cloud cover had been increasing for about an hour, yet the sky did not have that yellowish, lowering look that so often precedes a tornado. The trash now loaded onto the wagon, Elden started up the rider mower and drove slowly down the road toward the west edge of Lakeview Hills. At the edge of the property he turned the rider mower southward onto the path that wound over the hill and between the cornfield and a thin line of trees along the west edge of the farm. Crossing the crest of the hill, he followed the path as it slanted back eastward between a thicket and the cornfield. At the bottom of the hill Elden at last reached his destination — the trash dump. He pulled the wagon in front of the trash dump and put the rider mower in neutral. He then began unloading the trash from the wagon. As Elden was busy unloading the trash, he did not see anything of what was unfolding behind him.

No more had Elden commenced his descent down the backside of the hill to the trash dump than the weather commenced deteriorating rapidly. The clouds began turning ominously dark, the wind started to pick up, and then that yellowish hue that so often precedes a tornado crept over the sky to the west. The sound of the wind gently rustling through the trees was soon drowned out by the shrillness of this new wind whistling madly as it accelerated eastward. Suddenly there it was — a swirling funnel cloud less than a mile to the west! And it was whipping its way directly towards Lakeview Hills! In fact, the tornado was moving in a line to go directly toward the trash dump where Elden was still unloading trash from the wagon hooked to the back of the rider mower. Elden was in line to meet a tornado!

But Elden had no inkling of the ominous change in the weather. Busily unloading trash, he didn't notice the wind picking up. As he was on the backside of the hill, the increase in wind velocity didn't pierce his conscious mind for some time. And as he was facing toward the east while unloading the trash, he saw nothing of the tornado bearing down on him from the west. Terry Witt and Lester Anderson saw the storm first. Terry was working outside when he saw the funnel cloud heading straight for Lakeview Hills. Lester was also working outside when the tornado came into his view. Independently of each other, they both saw the powerful storm bearing down on Lakeview Hills at approximately the same time. As they spread the news of the impending storm, someone switched on the alarm siren to warn everyone a tornado was approaching. On the backside of the hill Elden finished unloading the trash from the wagon and started the slow ride back to the community shop. Because of the noise generated by the rider mower, Elden never heard the alarm siren.

But not all the eyes watching this tornado were human eyes. Yahweh Almighty was looking down from heaven. And Elden's prayers came into His mind.

Just before he ducked into the tornado shelter, Terry Witt looked again at the whirlwind as it approached Lakeview

Hills. Then he saw it happen — the tornado split in two! One of the new tornadoes turned abruptly and headed toward the south while the other new tornado veered sharply and swirled toward the north! Neither funnel cloud crossed Lakeview Hills! One of the new tornadoes skirted the property to the south while the other one went around it to the north.

By then Elden had realized that the weather had turned ugly. He accelerated the rider mower to return to the shop as quickly as possible. But by the time he ascended the crest of the hill Yahweh had already split the original tornado into two tornadoes and sent them both packing!

When Elden returned from unloading the trash, Terry Witt and Lester Anderson met him and told him what had just happened. Elden was amazed and glorified Yahweh for His protection. Then they all thanked Yahweh together. Elden had prayed that Yahweh would stop any tornado in its tracks. Yahweh did that and more! He split the tornado in two!

CHAPTER TWO

HILLBILLY HEAVEN

Elden Shisler was born June 30th, 1931 near Novinger, Missouri. Born at home, his grandmother Shisler, a part-time midwife, assisted in his entrance into this world. The youngest of four children born to Alfred Eugene and Rhoda Shisler, Elden was preceded into this life by his brother Alfred Leon, his sister Lillie, and his sister Oliva. The family would have included six children, but twin sisters who came before Elden died at childbirth.

Northern Missouri in 1931 was nothing like the world we know today. Elden's early childhood was spent in a world in which there was as much of 19th Century life as there was of 20th Century life. The world was changing rapidly at the time; however, in Northern Missouri the pace of change was much slower than it was in New York or California.

Elden grew up on a farm — a farm that the modern world had only begun to reach. Of course, his father Alfred Eugene was a farmer; in fact he was somewhat of a sharecropper. Alfred farmed the land on which he lived with a horse-drawn plow, a harrow, and a cultivator. He primarily raised corn which he planted with a horse-drawn corn planter. The whole family harvested the crop by hand. At the end of each harvest the corn and other crops were sold for money to buy feed for their animals, seed for the next year's crop, and the other things the Shislers needed for their meager existence.

Elden recalls that the Shisler family always had a big garden. Lettuce, tomatoes, blackeyed peas, you name it — if it was a vegetable that grew in Northern Missouri soil, it was probably to be found in the Shisler' s garden. So, of course, vegetables were always a staple of the family diet. In addition, the Shislers had horses, cows, and chickens on their small farm. Naturally the horses were not part of their Spartan diet; rather, they were draft animals to perform the labor of dragging the Shisler's soon-to-be outmoded farm equipment behind them. The children were taught to milk one of the cows at an early age; so the Shisler family always had fresh (albeit unpasteurized) milk to drink. Chicken and eggs were also staples of the diet in the Shisler household.

Let's look at their diet another way. Since they grew most of their own food, the Shislers purchased very little of what they ate at a grocery store or even a farm market. In other words, their diet included almost no processed foods. They didn't eat boxed breakfast cereals as we do nor did their diet include canned or frozen meats, canned or frozen vegetables, nor virtually any food that had been processed and then put in a box or can. No Wheaties, no Cheerios, no lasagna (canned or otherwise), no Tater Tots! Of course, some of these items hadn't been invented yet; nevertheless, you get the point: the Shisler diet in the 1930's was nothing like the way that most Americans eat today.

Elden Shisler's training in the ways of farm life commenced at the tender age of 4. That was the age at which he learned to milk his first cow. Just like in those old Western movies, Elden would sit on a stool near the rear end of one side of the cow and squeeze her utters by hand until he finished milking the cow. Then he would tote the pail of milk to the place where it was to be stored. For a preschooler this was no small job. But if he wanted his breakfast, Elden had to milk the cow first. Milking the cow was done around 6 AM in the morning — well before breakfast.

Elden also learned to feed the chickens and gather their eggs at the age of 4. He would scatter feed throughout the chicken coop and then fill the chickens' basins with water. And then he would gather up their eggs and take them into the house. Cleaning up the chicken coop was also part of taking care of the chickens, but I will spare you a graphic description of that particular job.

A basic description of Elden's first home is in order at this point. Although his first house wasn't a cabin, in some ways it was more like a 19th Century cabin than a 20th Century house. In fact, when Elden initially described this house to me, the only houses in the 20th Century that came to mind were the shacks that existed in Appalachia up to about 1960.

Like all the rooms in the Shisler home, the living room had an old hardwood floor. There weren't too many splinters in the hardwood flooring, but it was best not to run through this room (or any other room in the house for that matter) - especially if a person didn't have his shoes on! The dominant piece of furniture in the living room was a sturdy wood chair that Elden's father Alfred Eugene had reclaimed by putting a new hickory bark seat on it. In addition, there were enough other wooden chairs in the living room so that everyone in the family could sit down and visit together. There was neither a sofa nor a couch nor any other of the softer pieces of furniture that we have become accustomed to sitting on today. A few hardwood tables on which stood kerosene lamps completed the living room decor. TV hadn't been invented yet; the Shislers were too poor to purchase a radio,

The antiquated kitchen was dominated by two old-fashioned wood stoves - one for heating and one for cooking. The wood stove for heating was made out of tin with a cast iron bottom. Two to three inches of ashes had to be kept in the bottom of this wood stove at all times to keep the bottom from burning out. The cook stove was similar in design except that it had doors on either side of it so that you could look right through it if both doors were open at the same time. Elden specifically remembers that it had three cast iron legs and one wooden leg because one cast iron leg had been broken off. Needless to say, I consider it no small miracle that the Shislers managed to survive these somewhat hazardous stoves without either burning their humble abode down or burning themselves into eternity. Surely the Almighty watched over them even then.

The Shisler house had neither electricity nor running water; so a porcelain wash basin set on an old orange crate served as the kitchen sink. Of course, the Shislers didn't have a refrigerator; the basement under the house served as a semi-refrigerator. The milk that Elden squeezed out of the Shislers' milk cow each morning was put into stone crocks and stored in the basement. Meats, butter, cheese, and other perishables were also stored in the basement. Milk, of course, could not be kept for very long in this partial refrigeration, but since the Shislers had their own milk cow, that was never a problem. Vegetables they canned themselves were also stored in the basement. Completing the kitchen was a No. 3 Morse tub fashioned of galvanized metal; this was the family bathtub.

In the dining room the chief piece of furniture was a handmade oak dining table crafted by Elden's grandfather and then given to his family. A dish cabinet for storing their limited supply of dishes and glassware was also to be found in this room. Wooden chairs surrounding the oak dining table rounded out the furnishings in the dining room.

Two bedrooms completed Elden's first abode in this world. Elden's parents had one bedroom and Elden, his older brother, and his two sisters shared the other bedroom. No one slept alone. Alfred Eugene and Rhoda, of course, shared their marital bed. Elden's two sisters Lillie and Oliva slept in one bed while Elden and his older brother Alfred Leon also shared a bed. Today we complain about having to share a room with a brother or sister. How would we feel if we had to share our bed every night with our brother or sister? By the way, none of these beds were king-sized or even queen-sized. A twin bed at best is what everybody in the Shisler household had to share with somebody else. For the record, the Shisler beds were not Sealy Posturpedic; their beds were composed of straw mattresses on the bottom with hand-sewn goose feather mattresses on top. Pillows were also made of goose feathers. I have a vivid picture in my mind of what pillow fights between the children must have looked like in the Shisler household.

So the old wood-framed house that the Shisler family rented from Elden's uncle (his father Alfred Eugene's brother) consisted of five rooms all on one floor. In case you haven't noticed by now, that means the Shislers were missing a room that none of us would think of doing without: the Shisler home didn't have a bathroom! The outhouse was outside almost 100 feet from the house! Many times on a cold January evening Elden recalls putting on a coat to make a trek to the outhouse and then sitting there shivering while doing what we all have to do. Moreover, the outhouse didn't have a space heater or even its own wood stove; about the best that can be said for it is that it got its occupant out of the wind (I mean the wind outside). Now you're probably wondering why people back then didn't locate the outhouse closer to the house so that folks didn't freeze their you-know-what off just getting there. Again I think this was a matter of wind. Imagine if the outhouse had only been 10 feet from the house and the wind blew by the outhouse first before blowing by the house! There were enough smells to deal with in houses without refrigeration without compounding the problem. (And sanitation is yet another matter regarding outhouses that we won't address here.) So you get the picture — and the scent! Elden's first home didn't smell anything like the homes we live in today — not by a long shot!

Before leaving Elden's first house, let's return to the fact that it had neither indoor plumbing nor running water. The Shislers had an open well next to their house. Actually it was a cistern well: rainwater ran off the roof into the eave troughs (what we now call gutters) and from the troughs flowed down into the well. Still the well was deep enough that you had to use a chain and bucket to draw water out of it. All the water used in the Shisler home was drawn from this cistern well. First, the water was poured through a cloth to purify it and then it was boiled to sterilize it to some degree. Milk from their milk cow was similarly strained through a cloth to purify it.

The farm that Alfred Shisler rented from his brother was only 40 acres, but that was more than enough land to take care of when your tractors were horses. Besides the farmhouse the Shisler farm included a small barn for housing the animals and a chicken coop. A 50 foot square pond served as a watering hole for their horses and cows.

Besides their everyday life in eking out an existence on their meager farm, the Shislers had one important activity which they did every week. That activity was attending the Seventh Day Church of God every Saturday. Everyone went to his or her particular Sabbath school class first for about half an hour and then the whole family participated in the worship service together that started every Saturday at 1 PM. The worship service commenced with the children's meeting in which Bible verse recitation by the children and singing were the main activities. The main worship service with hymns, prayer, and the preaching of the Word then ensued. Whatever the Shislers lacked in this world's goods, they felt they had much more in the hope they had in Jesus Christ and His Word.

Moreover, this weekly devotion to Almighty God carried over into their daily life. Alfred Eugene Shisler led his family in devotions on a daily basis. Devotions were simple: they always consisted of Scripture reading and prayer. Alfred Eugene gave no options on devotions; everyone in his household had to be there.

Such was the world into which Elden Shisler came— a world short on the amenities of this life, but long on faith both for this world and for the world to come. When I think about this world, I think about the Mountain Dew commercials of over 30 years ago with all the cartoon hillbillies running around. Elden grew up a hillbilly in a hillbilly household; all of his roots are in these hillbilly beginnings. But the enduring image I have of the world in which Elden grew up is not an image of cartoon hillbillies jumping around to a lot of mountain music. Rather, it is the image of Gary Cooper and Walter Brennan in the movie "Sergeant York" in the scene where Sergeant York comes to grips with his sins and gives his heart to the Lord. Hillbilly Heaven is an apt description of this world.

CHAPTER THREE

A CHILD IN THE SHOW ME STATE

In spite of the fact that we are all born at age 0, many people have actually insisted that real life begins at a certain age — be that 5 or 18 or 21 or whatever age they surmise. In the farmland of Northern Missouri in the 1930's real life began at age 4. You see that's when life as all play and no work came to an end. To eke out their meager existence everyone in the Shisler household had to do their part. That meant work!

Besides picking up his toys, Elden had already been given the jobs of milking a cow and taking care of the chickens at age 4. But that's not all! Soon after Elden's baptism into the family chores, he was given another one — carrying in wood for the wood stoves. Elden is not exactly sure whether toting in firewood started at age 4 or age 5, but it was well before he reached age 6. He had to fetch the firewood from the woodpile outside their house and then stack it neatly on the floor near the wood stoves in the kitchen. Sometimes he got a little help from his older brother with this chore, but not always.

One chore that Elden escaped until he was school age was chopping holes in the ice on the family pond during the winter time. The holes had to be big enough so that the cows could get their faces into the water and take a drink. Elden remembers many a cold winter day on which his father tediously chopped holes in the ice so that the Shislers' cows could have water to drink.

Another memory Elden has of the winter time during his childhood is that of his father making ice cleats. Alfred Eugene took metal pieces out of old mowing machines, heated them on the wood stove, and then bent the heated pieces into ice cleats. The end result was that everyone in the family had ice cleats which they could wear outside on icy winter days for extra traction in walking around.

Gardening was really secondary farm education for Elden. He didn't start to learn gardening until age 8! First, he was taught to hoe weeds out of the corn. Then he learned how to weed the vegetable garden. Lessons in harvesting the vegetables by hand followed. At age 9 or 10 Elden was taught how to harness a horse to the horse-drawn farm equipment used in the family farming. Lastly, he learned how to manage a horse and whatever piece of farm equipment the horse was dragging behind him.

Elden started school at age 7 rather than age 6 because the school building was too far away for a six-year-old to walk to every day. Elden recalls his first schoolhouse well: it was a one-room stuccoed schoolhouse with a hardwood floor and a pot-bellied wood stove in the middle of the room. The desks were slightly more modern: they had wooden tops with metal bottoms. A high ceiling and spare furnishings complete the picture of Elden's first school.

Grades 1-8 all met simultaneously in this one-room school. Generally there were around forty students, but there was only one teacher. One teacher for eight grades! Lesson planning was quite difficult for a teacher the first year of teaching in this situation, but afterwards she could use the same lesson plans year after year. Elden attended this school for five years. Reading, writing, and arithmetic were the primary subjects, but Elden also recalls learning some history and science.

For Elden, however, schooling at home had commenced at age 5 — about two years before he began his formal education. Elden's father Alfred Eugene taught him both his ABC's and his numbers before he ever went to a public school. When Elden actually got into school, he remembers his dad helping him with his spelling and his multiplication. His father also taught him reading at home from the first year that he attended the one-room school. The textbook for this home reading instruction was almost always the Bible.

To complete this picture of Elden's early years, a description of a typical weekday will suffice. Elden generally got up around 6 AM. He dressed and did his chores with the chickens and the milk cow first. Then he sat down with his family for breakfast. Around 7 AM he departed for the one-room school — an hour's walk away! School commenced promptly at 8 AM and didn't conclude until 4 PM. Of course, school time was dominated by the aforementioned reading, writing, and arithmetic with some time mixed in for recess, lunch, and the other subjects of education. Elden left school at 4 PM and walked an hour to get home. Upon his arrival at home, he again had to do his chores with the animals. The Shisler family typically ate supper together around 6 PM. Devotions followed supper; homework followed devotions. Bedtime was at 8 PM when Elden was younger—then a little later as he grew older.

The Bible for a textbook! Family devotions every evening immediately after supper! From the beginning Elden's life was one with strong spiritual overtones. Even as a small child he recalls his parents talking to him about the Lord. Elden's father Alfred Eugene in particular shared with his son often about his sinful nature, Jesus' death on the cross for his sins, and Jesus' plan of salvation for his life. But that brings us to Elden's spiritual life and hence our next chapter.

CHAPTER FOUR

SUFFER THE LITTLE CHILDREN

The day was September 9th, 1939 — a day best remembered in history for the Nazi Blitzkrieg of Poland. But Northern Missouri in 1939 was a long way (and maybe a few light years away) from war-torn Europe at the beginning of World War II. On this particular day 8-year-old Elden Shisler had what was for him a much more important concern — the salvation of his soul!

Elden's father had been talking to him for some time about the Lord's plan of salvation for his life. Alfred Eugene had shared with his son about his sinful nature and his need for a Savior to redeem him from his sins. Moreover, he had told Elden how Jesus had died on the cross for the sins of the whole world and for his sins in particular. Finally, he had shared with his son that if he would give his heart and life to Jesus, Jesus would come into his heart and save him from his sins.

On September 9th, 1939 Elden came under the conviction of the Holy Spirit. He then knew in his heart that he was a sinner and realized that Jesus Christ was the only answer for his sin. His father recognized the Holy Spirit working on his son's heart and asked him whether he knew the difference between right and wrong; Elden replied in the affirmative. Then Alfred Eugene asked Elden if he wanted to get saved — specifically, if he wanted to invite Jesus into his heart and life. He again shared with his son the whole plan of salvation — the penalty for sin, repentance from sin, and Jesus Christ as the only answer to sin.

Elden hesitated at first; he then told his dad that he wasn't sure he was ready. Alfred Eugene replied by counseling his son to take his time and think everything over. After a pause he added that the Holy Spirit only gives each of us a certain number of opportunities to get saved. Finally, he admonished Elden that if he put this decision off, the next time it would be more difficult. Five to ten minutes later Elden made the decision to get saved. From the moment he made the decision he felt the presence of the Holy Spirit. Elden then prayed with his father, repenting of his sins and inviting Jesus Christ into his heart and life. The presence of the Lord immediately flooded his heart! To use Elden's manner of speech, he then knew that he knew that he knew he was saved!

That same afternoon Elden was immersed in the waters of baptism in a neighbor's pond. Elden felt clean when he came up out of the waters of baptism. His sins were indeed forgiven; he felt as if a great weight had been lifted off his heart.

Not long after getting saved Elden remembers praying one day that he would walk with Jesus. Elden admits that he has strayed from walking with Jesus a few times in his life. But his backslidings have never lasted long; Jesus has always returned him to the straight and narrow way and his walk with Him. Elden prayed this prayer when he was 8 years old. He is now in his 70's and the Lord has been answering this prayer all his life.

When Elden was age 9, he prayed to hear the Lord's voice. About 6 months after praying this prayer, Elden was outside in the yard playing one day. Suddenly he heard a voice calling out loud, "Elden!" He thought the voice sounded like his dad's voice. However, Elden knew that his father had gone to town to buy some groceries. But being certain that it was his dad's voice he was hearing, Elden walked up the path from the Shisler home toward the road looking for his father. He then saw his dad walking towards him from the opposite direction. "Dad!' he yelled out, "You called me." "No, my son, I didn't call you," Alfred Eugene replied. Elden then told his father about the voice that had called him by name. His father counseled him that he had undoubtedly heard the voice of the Lord. Read I Samuel 3: God spoke to Elden in much the same manner that he spoke to Samuel.

About 6 months after the above experience, Elden had another experience with hearing the audible voice of the Lord. One day he was outside playing on his stick horse. Although his stick horse was not at all alive and every bit just a toy, he was very real to imaginative young Elden. Suddenly something came over Elden and he became very angry at his stick horse. In fact, he got so angry that he began swearing at his stick horse. In the middle of a curse word the Lord spoke to him again, "Elden!" When Elden heard the Lord's voice, he felt like a shockwave went right through him! Then the Lord asked him, "What did you accomplish by swearing?" "Nothing," Elden stammered meekly. He felt very convicted. Elden stopped swearing and has almost never sworn since.

When Elden was 13 years old, he had a third experience with the audible voice of the Lord. His folks were getting ready to go to the store. His mother had just put some cornbread in the oven to bake and she asked Elden to watch it while they were gone to the store. Naturally Elden said that he would and then his parents left for their shopping trip. Being a very normal 13-year-old boy, Elden went outside to play and forgot all about the cornbread baking in the oven. Suddenly the Lord spoke his name, "Elden!" As when he was younger, Elden again thought that his father had called him. Moreover, the voice from seemingly out-of-nowhere brought

Elden back to his full senses and it immediately dawned on him to check on the cornbread in the oven. He ran into the house and checked on the cornbread; it was cooking fine and not burning. Elden then stuck with the cornbread until it was done and he took it out of the oven. As the cornbread finished cooking, Elden realized that his dad wasn't home; so he couldn't have heard his father calling him. When he was 9 years old, Elden had prayed to hear the Lord's voice. God had answered him 3 times!

As with most of his early spiritual life, Elden's father was his teacher in the area of prayer. Elden was first taught to give the blessing before meals when he was age 7. He was also taught to pray in family devotions. In these brief meetings each member of the family took a turn praying. The way Elden was taught to pray was very simple: just talk to the heavenly Father the same way you talk to anybody else — only with great respect.

Elden started praying regularly on his own when he was age 9. Alfred Eugene had taught him that he could talk to his heavenly Father whenever he wanted to; so Elden did. It is the habit that has shaped his whole life. In the beginning Elden prayed for his family, his relatives, and his friends. He also prayed for people he knew that were unsaved. Elden still does all of this, but now he prays for the whole church and the whole world. Mustard seeds grow; the Bible says so. Elden is one of those mustard seeds. His prayers grow and the answers are still coming.

CHAPTER FIVE

PIGEONS AND HORSES

Pigeons were plentiful in Northern Missouri in the 1930's and 1940's. Of course, these pigeons were not passenger pigeons; they had already been extinct for quite some time. These were just regular ol' pigeons. Moreover, they were wild pigeons unless you caught them and put them in a cage.

Elden had already kept some pigeons, but he didn't catch his first pigeons himself. His father had given them to him. They were kept in a loft in the barn. However, the problem with pigeons in barn lofts is simple: where pigeons go, cats also go. Needless to say, stray cats caught Elden's first pigeons and devoured them. But Elden had become somewhat attached to his pigeons; he missed them. So Elden asked his father if he could catch some pigeons and keep them for himself. Alfred Eugene, of course, gave his son permission.

So 10-year-old Elden prayed to the Lord that he would catch some wild pigeons. Shooting pigeons has always been pretty easy, but catching them is not so easy, particularly if you're trying to do so by yourself. About one week after praying his prayer to catch some wild pigeons, Elden caught his first pigeon in the loft of his family dentist's barn. Then he caught some more at the Shislers' landlord's barn. Elden remembers thanking the Lord for answering his prayer.

When Elden was age 12, he prayed to get his own horse. Now this may seem like a strange prayer for the year 1943, but more people in Northern Missouri in 1943 were still traveling around on horses than in automobiles. Cars really didn't take over as the dominant means of transportation there until the late 1940's. Of course, Elden was saving his allowance money toward the purchase of his own horse. In addition, he was saving money that relatives gave him to buy candy. By the time Elden was 13 he had almost saved enough money to purchase a horse. Then his father chipped in the little bit that he was short and Elden bought his own horse. The year was 1944; Elden paid $275 for his horse. (That would be over $1,000 in today's money.) For a 13-year-old boy this was an amazing answer to prayer!

Elden's horse was nothing special—just an 8-year-old mare weighing about 1200 pounds. But this horse was very special to Elden. Once Elden got his own horse he didn't have to walk to school any more; from then on he rode his horse to school.

Moreover, once Elden got his own horse he didn't stop praying there. Next he prayed for a harness and somebody gave him one. Then he prayed for a buggy and he was able to buy one for only $15 (which Elden tells me was a very low price at the time).

One day when Elden was age 14, Alfred Eugene was greasing the family buggy outside while Elden was down at the barn taking care of his pigeons. Suddenly he heard a voice speak distinctly, "Elden!" As in the experiences I have related to you previously, Elden thought that his dad was calling him. So Elden left the barn and found his dad. "Father, did you call me?" he queried. "No, my son," Alfred Eugene replied. So Elden returned to the barn and resumed taking care of his pigeons. No more had he done so than he heard the voice again, "Elden!" Once again Elden left the barn and returned to where his father was greasing the buggy. "Father, did you call me?" Alfred Eugene again responded, "No." Then his father perceived that the Lord might be speaking to his son again. So Alfred Eugene told Elden that what was happening to him might be similar to what happened to the boy Samuel in the Bible. He instructed his son that if the Lord spoke to him again, he should reply like Samuel: "Speak! For your servant heareth!" Elden returned to the barn, but he did not hear the Lord speak audibly again.

The Bible tells us: "For every beast of the forest is mine, and the cattle upon a thousand hills." (Psalms 50:10) I'm sure that included a few pigeons and a horse. Jesus promised, "My sheep hear my voice." (John 10:27) I've always taken that to mean that the Lord speaks to my heart. For a child in Northern Missouri, however, the Lord did something very special; he spoke to Elden audibly — the child who prayed to hear His voice!

CHAPTER SIX

A DIFFICULT EDUCATION

In contrast to his relatively happy life at home, Elden's life at school was filled with uneasiness and failure. Elden completed the eighth grade, but never finished high school. In fact, school for Elden was the trial of his early life. Now Elden was neither mentally deficient nor mentally handicapped, but neither was he mentally gifted in any way. The truth is that when it came to public education, Elden was almost always somewhat below average. To put it another way, when it came to book learning, what was easy for others was indeed difficult for Elden.

How difficult was education for Elden? Elden actually failed to pass grade levels in school 3 times! Now I'm not talking about high school or college here: Elden failed to pass a grade level in primary school (grades 1-8) 3 times. The failure in school itself was difficult enough for a not-so-gifted youth to deal with, but then there were the taunts and ridicule of his classmates to deal with as well. Of course, if Elden had been a stocky, muscular kid, he could have just punched the teasers out. Elden, however, was more on the skinny side and totally lacking in rippling muscles. So all he could do was just bear the taunting and cry inside. The whole educational experience was so difficult for Elden that around age 10 he started praying for passing grades. This is one of the few prayers Elden ever prayed that was not totally answered.

On top of everything mentioned above, Elden was not a healthy boy during his primary school years. He frequently suffered from fainting and blackout spells. According to his doctors, these fainting spells were primarily due to leakage from his heart. Of course, Elden and his parents prayed that the Lord would heal him; in time his condition improved and the fainting and blackout spells occurred less and less often. Eventually their prayers were answered and the fainting spells stopped altogether. But these spells were no help to a boy already struggling with his education.

What happened with the fainting spells was that Elden missed a lot of school because of his condition. Of course, missed schooling meant missed assignments, missed homework, and missed exams. Elden's parents attempted to help him keep up with his schoolwork at home during the periods of his home recoveries. However, for someone who already found book learning as difficult as Elden did, the lost school time in the aftermath of fainting spells was more often than not too much to overcome. Elden's sickness was a major factor in his failing to pass 3 grade levels in school.

When Elden reached age 16, he finally got a teacher in school who really helped him. George Campbell took young Elden under his wing and put the extra effort into helping him that none of his predecessors had. He even tutored his struggling pupil many afternoons after school when all the other students had gone home. With George's patient help reading, writing, and arithmetic were slightly smaller mountains than they had been before. George Campbell taught and tutored Elden Shisler for 2 years. Under his capable guidance Elden passed both the seventh and eighth grades and at last completed grammar school. He was 17 years old — long past the age for completing grammar school.

After starting to pray that he would get passing grades in school, Elden actually flunked two more grades levels. But Elden did not give up praying and eventually his prayers to finish grammar school were answered. Moreover, he was able to finish without much taunting from his classmates. As a 17-year-old graduating with a bunch of 14-year-olds, Elden was now the biggest kid in school.

Elden's educational trauma should give us some cause for reflection. He never made the dean's list nor won any academic awards. He finally went on to high school, but never got a high school diploma. I'm sure there wasn't anybody who ever thought Elden Shisler would do much of anything with his life. Nobody saw much in young Elden's future. Nobody but the Almighty!

CHAPTER SEVEN

SPRINGVALE

Before going ahead to Elden's brief tenure in high school, I want to tell you about an incident in his life that happened around the time he was finishing grammar school. In 1948 the world was just 2 years out of World War II. In the victorious United States patriotism ran high. Nevertheless, in China and Korea the forces of Communism were on the move. Even with the defeat of the Nazis, Communism meant that much of the world was still not safe for democracy. So Uncle Sam called upon young men to serve their country and make the world safe for democracy.

In this atmosphere of patriotism Elden Shisler was praying whether he should volunteer and go into the armed services or not. He prayed specifically that if he wasn't supposed to go, God would give him a sign. Elden prayed this prayer more than once. A few months later Elden was praying on an overcast evening. It was that twilight time of the evening just before sunset, yet there was enough light to make out the clouds that completely covered the sky overhead. The sky was so overcast that not a ray of sunlight penetrated the clouds. In the house where Elden was praying the lights had not yet been turned on for the evening. Suddenly a yellowish light about the size of a softball appeared on the wall opposite where Elden was praying. As Elden continued to pray, he kept looking at the light directly across from him. There were no lamps where the yellowish light appeared, yet it continued to glow. The light remained there glowing for about ten minutes. Finally, Elden raised his hands to the Lord and the light disappeared. Elden took this supernatural light as the sign he had prayed for. Specifically, he took this sign as the Lord's answer that he was not supposed to go into the armed services.

Now the United States military had a draft at that time. If they didn't get enough volunteers, they simply drafted the extra manpower they needed. So when Elden reached age 18, he was classified by the Selective Service 1-A — the most eligible draft classification. Elden then filled out a conscientious objector form and was reclassified by the Selective Service 4-E. Later he was still called in for an examination after which he was again reclassified 101 — unsuitable for military duty. The sign was true: Elden Shisler never served in the United States armed services.

When Elden was 18 years old, his parents enrolled him at Springvale Academy in Owasso, Michigan. Springvale Academy is still in existence; it is a private high school run by the Seventh Day Church of God. Seventh Day Church of God members from all over the country send their teenagers to this Christian boarding school so that they can get a good high school education while also learning the doctrines of the Seventh Day Church of God. There were only about forty students when Elden enrolled in Springvale Academy. Elden attended school there for 2 years, but never completed a high school education. The first year he attended Springvale his subjects included Bible I, English grammar, algebra I, world history, general science, agriculture, and physical education. The second year he took Bible II, American literature, algebra II, typing, advanced general science, agriculture, and physical education. With the exceptions of Bible and agriculture the curriculum was very similar to that taught in the public schools. As always, book learning was difficult for Elden, but with no more fainting spells to deal with he at least struggled through and passed all his courses.

Agriculture was a big part of Springvale's curriculum when Elden attended there. In addition to classroom instruction in agriculture, every student had agricultural jobs to do on the 146 acre farm where Springvale Academy was situated. Elden's primary job was feeding and taking care of 500 chickens, but at least that was a job his early years had prepared him for. In addition, he had to milk four cows every morning and evening as well as throw down silage for the cows to eat. Finally, he had to feed and care for two horses. Thus, a typical day at Springvale would involve chores both before and after school.

Being a small private school, Springvale Academy didn't have a lot of buildings. The main building had all the school's classrooms on its first and second floors and the girls' dormitory on its third floor. The boys' dormitory was in a separate army-barracks type building not far from the main building. Of course, there were barns for the farm animals and coops for the chickens and a few buildings for the farm's equipment. Education certainly has changed in the fifty plus years since Elden went to school.

Elden had a buddy at Springvale, his roommate Clifford Tuttle. Also a farm boy, Clifford was the right roommate for Elden. In fact, during Elden's second year at Springvale he and Clifford had their own special project together with three other students — growing and tending their own cucumber patch. Now when Elden first told me about this, I thought to myself that this cucumber patch project must have been a sack job for a bunch of farm boys. I thought so until he told me that their cucumber patch was five acres! Now that is a cucumber patch! Elden and his classmates were growing five acres of cucumbers for a local canning plant. The farm manager tilled the ground for their cucumber patch and planted the seed for them, but after that it was their baby except for some early weeding by the farm manager. Elden and his classmates checked their patch for bugs and pests and got rid of any they found. Finally, they harvested the whole five acres of cucumbers by hand! Needless to say, I'm glad this was Elden's high school project and not mine.

I need to add at this point that above all Springvale Academy was a religious school. All the students met together every day for devotions before classes commenced. Elden remembers that all the students prayed that the chickens would produce well and they did. Moreover, the student body prayed that the crops would produce a bountiful harvest and they did. Personally Elden prayed to do better in school than he had ever done before and he did; Elden passed all his courses at Springvale — all of them. This was no mean accomplishment for someone who had experienced such difficulty in school as Elden had in primary school.

Near the end of his second year at Springvale, Elden and Clifford were in their room together one evening about bedtime. In fact, they were both in their bunks (Elden had the bottom bunk) with the lights turned off. Yet not long after the lights were turned off a light flooded all over the room as they lay in their bunks. Elden felt the Holy Spirit began speaking to his heart: "Your school days are over. You are needed back home in your local church. There is trouble." After he felt the Holy Spirit stop speaking, the room was dark again. Elden concluded the Lord wanted him to return home. So he dropped out of high school and returned to Northern Missouri. Interestingly there was trouble in his local church. Within a year of his return the church split into two separate groups.

Now in case this isn't obvious by now, while Elden Shisler was struggling through his public education, he was getting another education not designed by man. The Lord spoke to him as a boy and continued to speak to him as he grew up. Furthermore, from an early age Elden was taught to pray. As he continued to pray and saw his prayers answered, his faith grew. So he prayed more and saw his prayers answered more and of course his faith grew more. The Lord God was educating Elden for a task few men have succeeded at — the Lord was making Elden into a prayer warrior. "For ye see your calling, brethren, how that not many wise men after the flesh, not many mighty, not many noble, are called: But God hath chosen the foolish things of the world to confound the wise; and God hath chosen the weak things of the world to confound the things which are mighty; And base things of the world, and things which are despised hath God chosen, yea, and things which are not, to bring to nought things that are." (I Corinthians 1:26-28)

CHAPTER EIGHT

JOB STRUGGLES

—⋙—

Soon after his return from Michigan to Missouri, Elden's family moved from his boyhood home near Novinger to Milan, a town of almost 2,000 people about 20 miles away. Elden moved with them. For a young man who had lived on a farm all his life moving to Milan was almost like moving to a big city. Elden quickly made friends with most of his neighbors; although they lived in town, they were mostly country people like Elden and his family. However, boyhood in an outmoded farm operation and Elden's poor education had not prepared him for any career in life.

Of course, the 1950's were the decade when Elden was in his twenties. It was that time of life when young men explore their world and try to find their place in life. For many it was also that time of life when they sowed their wild oats. For a young man raised in a Bible-believing family, however, sowing his wild oats was never a consideration for Elden. If stud was a word in his vocabulary at the time, it was simply a board used in construction.

The summer after Elden returned to Missouri from Springvale he worked in a hayfield. Believe it or not, the farmer was still not using a tractor. In the hayfield Elden "ran" a ricker horse to harvest hay. At this point in the hay harvest the hay had already been cut. Elden harnessed the horse to a ricker that the horse pulled behind him. As the horse moved forward, the ricker pulled up the hay that had already been cut so that two guys walking behind the ricker could stack it up. Elden's job was to walk beside the horse and control the horse's movements so that the horse went straight through each row as the other two men harvested and stacked the hay.

During the next couple of years Elden didn't have regular work. Of course, he worked for neighboring farmers whenever he could helping with planting and harvesting. During the winter and occasionally during the summer he did some woodcutting. Actually Elden did all the odd jobs that he could find in the area where he lived. But odd jobs were no way to make a real living. So Elden prayed for work.

Finally, he answered an ad in a Seventh Day Church of God publication and the farmer who ran the ad hired him. So Elden moved to Roscoe, South Dakota and went to work for his fellow church member Matt Forkol. The job was simple: he was the farmer's helper and did whatever needed to be done to help raise the farmer's crops and take care of the farmer's animals. Here Elden learned how to run a tractor in a modern farm operation. Elden, however, did not learn to run the tractor and other mechanized farm equipment well enough to satisfy Matt Forkol. After about one year Matt Forkol let Elden go.

Elden did have a couple of good experiences while in the Seventh Day Church of God in Roscoe, South Dakota. For one thing Elden had learned to play the harmonica while growing up. Some of Matt Forkol's children had also learned to play the harmonica. Elden recalls playing his harmonica with the Forkol children a few times in church and everyone really enjoying all the harmonicas playing together in harmony. Elden also remembers one time when he was asked to give the sermon in church and was allotted

30 minutes in which to do so. Elden, however, only gave a 15 minute sermonette and then sat down. The elder in charge was so shocked that he asked Elden if he was already done. Since Elden felt that the Holy Spirit anointing had lifted at that point, he replied that he was indeed done.

After being let go by Mart Forkol, Elden once again returned home to Milan and lived with his folks. By then his father Alfred Eugene was no longer farming. As both of his parents were beginning to have some health problems, Elden then helped prepare meals for and take care of his parents. There was one notable event that occurred in Elden's life during this time period, but we will leave that for the next chapter. As before, Elden did farm work and other odd jobs to make some ready cash. But also as before, odd jobs were no way to make a real living. So once again Elden prayed for work.

God again answered Elden's prayers for regular work through an ad in a Seventh Day Church of God publication. Elden was hired to be trained as a plumber's apprentice. Fellow church member Raymond Smith hired him as his apprentice and helped Elden move to Fort Morgan, Colorado. The year was 1956. Ike was President, Communists were the bad guys, and Interstate highways were on the drawing boards. And Elden was in Colorado apprenticing in plumbing. Elden just didn't catch onto plumbing very well, but Raymond Smith was a conscientious Christian who didn't want to leave his fellow church member out in the cold. He kept his eyes open for something that Elden might do better and finally referred him to a building contractor.

The contractor whom Elden went to work for built houses. On this job Elden was taught to mix concrete for pouring foundations. This was his job the remainder of that year. Later Elden was also taught to nail up frames for houses. In the winter when housing construction in Colorado ceased, Elden shoveled sidewalks by hand to make a living. Since he then lived in the Colorado Rockies, there was plenty of snow to shovel during the Colorado winter. So this was a good, although strenuous way to make a living.

While in Fort Morgan, Elden of course attended the Seventh Day Church of God there. One day there arose a heated disagreement in the church that Elden was attending. People were arguing back and forth and tempers were heating up. The whole disagreement caused a great stir and confusion among the people present. In the midst of this disagreement Elden felt moved by the Holy Spirit to go up to the altar and pray. Soon other people came up and joined him at the altar. Not long afterwards the church grew still; all those who were arguing stopped arguing and fell silent. After people prayed for a while, one of the elders stood up and commended Elden for what he had done. After church virtually everybody shook Elden's hand. Elden recalls that there were no more arguments in that church while he attended there.

After about a year Elden decided that life in Colorado wasn't the life for him. So he again returned to Missouri and once again lived with his parents. As should be obvious from Elden's experiences in South Dakota and Colorado, Elden faithfully attended the Seventh Day Church of God throughout his twenties. During the 1950's Elden repeatedly had to pray for work and God always answered his prayers with some type of job. Many of these jobs were seasonal, but for Elden they were God's provision. "Give us this day thy daily bread" is a prayer that many of us have learned to pray by memory. For many people, however, it has become nothing more than a vain repetition. For Elden Shisler this prayer was often for his next meal.

CHAPTER NINE

AN ANGELIC PILLOW

The year was 1955. The Russians had spread the net of Communism over Eastern Europe. Television had supplanted radio as the mainstay of home entertainment. And Dwight Eisenhower was President of the United States. Although he had some access to television, none of these happenings were major events for Elden Shisler.

Elden was approaching 25 years of age and still hadn't found his niche in life. His brief adventure in South Dakota certainly hadn't turned into a career occupation. So Elden was back in Missouri doing odd jobs to make ends meet while helping his parents at home. Although his father Alfred Eugene had not been diagnosed with Parkinson's disease at this point in time, the symptoms of the oncoming disorder were already beginning to affect his movements. In this situation Elden with all his job problems in effect became the primary provider for the Shisler family.

What sort of jobs did Elden do? He primarily did the same sort of manual labor jobs that he had done all his life. He helped neighboring farmers with planting and harvesting their crops, helped bale hay, and helped cut wood during the winter months when there was no farm work to be done. He even ran a paper route for some period of time. With this temporary job syndrome young Elden's life was indeed a meager existence. The Shislers always had food on their table, but not much more.

One of the harvesting jobs that Elden did was assisting his neighbor Lee Reece with scooping harvested corn from a wagon into Lee's corn crib. One day in November of 1955 Elden was walking over to Lee Reece's farm to help with this corn transfer. As he left the country road that connected their farms and walked onto the driveway up to his neighbor's farmhouse, Lee's son Donnie turned onto the driveway driving the family tractor which was pulling a load of corn in a wagon hitched to the back of the tractor. Elden signaled to him and asked if he could hitch a ride up to his neighbor's corn crib. So Donnie stopped the tractor and invited Elden to stand on the tractor's running board for the brief ride up the driveway to the corn crib.

Now Donnie was at that wild stage of life where most things were done with complete abandon. Whether he imagined himself as a cowboy chasing the bad guys or as a horse trainer running his steed at faster and faster paces, no one will ever know. The fact is that he ran the tractor more like he was riding a wild horse than running a valuable piece of farm equipment. Tractor drag racing would have been a very good sport for him as he especially liked popping the clutch when he took off.

So Elden mounted the running board on the right side of the tractor and the adventure commenced. Donnie popped the clutch with such force that the tractor lurched forward as it accelerated down the driveway. The force of this lurching acceleration caused Elden to lose his balance and he tumbled off the tractor right in front of the oncoming wagon. Over his chest rolled the front wheel of the corn-filled wagon as his head was by then under the wagon. Elden was rolled onto his side by the time the back wheel of the wagon rolled over his face! Amazingly there was enough air remaining in Elden's lungs for him to scream for help. Donnie stopped the tractor and came running to where Elden lay. Elden moaned for him to get his father Lee. So Donnie left Elden helpless in the driveway and ran to get his father.

When Lee Reece pulled up in the family sedan, he and his son carefully picked up Elden and loaded him into the back seat. Then they took off for the area hospital in Milan. About fifteen minutes later they arrived at the hospital and Elden was rushed into the emergency room. Of course, he was given some medicine to help with the pain. Then x-rays were taken to see how many of his ribs were crushed and what other bones in his chest and face were broken. Moreover, the doctors wanted to see if there was any damage to any of his internal organs or any internal bleeding. When the doctors looked at the x-rays, they were amazed. Although there were fractures, not one rib nor bone in Elden's chest or face was broken. Not one! A wagon filled with over 60 bushels of corn had just run over Elden's chest and face and not a bone in his body was broken! Moreover, none of his internal organs were damaged and there was no evidence of any internal bleeding. Dr. E. W. Simpson and his medical staff were astounded. When Elden's neighbor had told them what had happened to Elden, they thought that his injuries would be so severe that they probably couldn't even save his life. Yet not a bone in his body was broken!

Dr. Simpson and his assistants went into Elden's hospital room to question Elden. "Did the wagon really run over you?" they asked. Elden replied, "Yes." "Right over your chest?" "Yes." "And the back wheel right over your face?" "Yes." "An accident like this should have crushed your chest and your face and possibly even have killed you, but we've looked at your x-rays and you don't have any broken bones. We don't know how this is possible." Then Elden responded, "I felt like there was a pillow between my chest and the wheel when the front wheel ran over me." "And what about your face?"

Dr. Simpson and his assistants inquired. "I felt like there was a pillow between my face and the back wheel too," Elden replied. "Well, this is truly amazing," they concluded. Thus the conversation at Elden's hospital bedside came to an end.

David "Ike" Chapman, one of Elden's closest friends in Milan, still remembers this accident 50 years later. He recollects, "Everyone around Milan said what a miracle it was that Elden wasn't hurt any worse than he was!"

Elden went on to recover from his injuries. In time all his fractures healed up and all the pain and discomfort went away. Elden had always prayed that God would protect him no matter what happened to him. On a November day in 1955 God answered Elden's prayer; He sent an angel who placed an angelic pillow between Elden and a wagon full of corn! "For he shall give his angels charge over thee, to keep thee in all thy ways. They shall bear thee up in their hands, lest thou dash thy foot against a stone. (Psalm 91:11-12)

CHAPTER TEN

HELEN OF STEWARTSVILLE

By 1960 Elden's father Alfred Eugene had been going downhill with Parkinson's disease for some time. During this time period Elden had been helping his parents at home while doing various jobs around Milan. With his deteriorating condition Alfred Eugene needed a great deal of assistance in taking care of himself. His wife Rhoda was able to do this to some degree until she fell and broke her hip. After that the primary burden for taking care of their parents fell on Elden and his sister Lillie. Of course, Lillie primarily took care of Rhoda while the task of tending to Alfred Eugene's needs fell upon Elden. Since his Parkinson's disease caused Alfred Eugene to shake so much, Elden had to help dress and feed his father as well as tend to his other personal needs.

Finally in 1961 Elden's father Alfred Eugene Shisler passed out of this life and went to meet the Lord. His father's death, of course, relieved Elden of the burden of caring for his father. His sister Lillie did most of the work in caring for their mother Rhoda; Elden only assisted his sister in taking care of their mother. By the time Alfred Eugene passed away, Rhoda was well on her way to becoming an invalid from the injuries that she sustained when she broke her hip. At that

THE PRAYER WARRIOR

point in time, however, she could still walk with assistance. But in 1965 Rhoda fell again and after that she could not walk any more. Not long afterwards her children had to put their mother in a nursing home because the burden of caring for her in her invalid state had simply become too great.

By this time things had improved for Elden somewhat in Milan. He had a regular job sweeping and cleaning the square in downtown Milan every evening except Sunday. At that time most of the businesses in Milan as well as the city offices and the police station were located on the downtown square. So there was plenty to do to clean up the square every evening after the normal people traffic there every day.

In fact, things had improved so much for Elden that after his father's death he was even able to buy his own house. It was a very small older house, but at least it was Elden's. As still a single man at the time Elden lived in this house during the first part of the 1960's. The house is no longer there as it finally deteriorated to the point that it was torn down.

Without the responsibility of caring for his father Elden also had more time to do something else that virtually all young men do - look for a wife. Elden was already in his 30's and still hadn't found the right woman. Naturally he had tried to find the right woman, but most of the women that he had asked out had just turned him down. Furthermore, among the few who dated him nothing had ever worked out. Either Elden and the young lady didn't have enough in common or Elden's lack of a solid career job was too much to provide a sense of security for the young lady. But Elden continued trying to find a wife; moreover, Elden prayed that the Lord would find him a wife.

Elden's church friend Barbara McClaren knew that Elden was looking for the right woman. One day she showed Elden a picture of her friend Helen Watkins. Elden was interested right away. However, Helen lived in Stewartsville, Missouri over 60 miles away from where Elden lived near

Milan, Missouri. For somebody like Elden who didn't have a good-paying job and thus didn't have a lot of money, he just couldn't afford to hop in the family car and drive over and meet Helen. So Elden started writing to Helen and she began writing back.

On about the fourth letter Elden asked Helen for a date. She wrote back and invited Elden to her house for the date. By then Elden had saved up enough money for a few trips to Stewartsville and back; so the date was set. On the appointed day Elden drove to Stewartsville. When he arrived at Helen's home, he first met her brother, sister, and parents. Then he went out to the backyard where Helen was hanging clothes on the clothesline to dry and met Helen. They sat down and visited for about an hour to get better acquainted. Elden really wanted to stay longer, but he had to go home and check on his invalid mother.

At this point I will do my best to describe Elden and Helen to you at that time in their lives. Elden was about 5 feet 8 inches tall, of average build, and weighed less than 160 pounds. His face has always looked rather weather-beaten, but probably not as much at 34 years of age. Moreover, Elden's ears have always seemed to point away from his head. If he had been a midget, he might have qualified for one of the seven dwarfs. Helen was just a little shorter than Elden — probably around 5 feet 6 inches tall and of a much stouter build than Elden. Her face was pudgy, but she had a pleasant smile.

From when they first met, there was definitely an attraction between Elden and Helen. For one thing Elden and Helen had many common religious beliefs. Both were born-again Christians and both were Sabbath keepers. Moreover, both of them had been taught to marry someone in the Christian faith. Plus their time clocks were ticking; both of them had tried to find a mate unsuccessfully for some period of time. I believe that they also genuinely enjoyed each other's company.

So for the next couple of months Elden continued seeing Helen every weekend. After about two months their relationship became quite serious. About a week before Christmas in 1965 Elden talked to Helen's parents about marrying their daughter and they gave their wholehearted consent. Then on Christmas Eve Elden Shisler proposed to Helen Watkins and she said "Yes" right away. Elden's prayer for a wife was being answered and Elden was very happy.

Right after Christmas the newly engaged couple commenced making wedding plans. Originally they planned to get married in June. However, in January an event would occur that would change their original plans. Elden was about to have another accident. And as always, his prayers for protection were in the mind of His heavenly Father.

CHAPTER ELEVEN

A CURVE IN THE ROAD

The time was during the third week of January in 1966. Elden had just spent the evening visiting with his new fiancee and had stayed quite late. In fact, it was almost 3 AM before he left and started the drive back home to Milan. Coming into Milan on Missouri State Highway 5 around 4:30 AM, weariness overtook Elden and he fell asleep at the wheel of his Ford custom V-8 sedan. Suddenly a bump in the road jolted him back to consciousness right before a sharp curve in the road. Elden realized that he would go off the road if he didn't negotiate the curve right in front of him. But being half asleep, Elden put his foot on the accelerator instead of the brake! His car left the road, jumped over a ditch, and headed straight for a Lee D-X oil storage building!

The D-X oil storage building was a facility where hundreds of barrels of oil were stored. If a moving vehicle were to crash into these barrels of oil, I am certain that both an explosion and a fire would have ensued. "Kaboom!" is the word used in the movies to describe such occurrences. Fortunately, the D-X storage facility had a solid concrete foundation about four feet high with sheet metal above the foundation.

The police were uncertain exactly how fast Elden was going when his car slammed into the D-X oil storage facility.

To jump over the ditch, however, he had to be going at least 50 miles per hour or his car wouldn't have cleared the ditch. Since he was on a state highway where most people usually drove 60 to 65 miles per hour, the best estimate is that he was going 60 to 70 miles per hour when he crashed into the D-X warehouse facility. Nevertheless, the foundation was too strong to give way even to a vehicle going over 60 miles per hour. Elden's car smashed into the concrete wall and then bounced back 20 feet! The radiator was meshed back into the engine and the driver-side door was jammed shut. The frame over the right wheel was bent like a rubber band. But Elden Shisler was still very much alive.

The newspaper account of the accident in the Milan Standard is as follows: "NAP CAUSES ACCIDENT - Elden Shisler, 34, of Milan suffered a fractured knee early Tuesday morning when his car went off the road on the corner south of the Cheese Factory, going across a ditch, and hitting the Lee D-X warehouse building and bouncing back approximately 20 feet. Shisler told Sheriff Bill Crowdis he thought he dozed off as he was coming into the curve from the west and was unable to keep the car under control. The time of the accident was 4:30 AM." (Reprinted with permission of the Milan Standard)

Elden remembers hitting the steering wheel before being knocked unconscious. His right kneecap was broken in a triangle shape, but he had no other major injuries. Of course, he was banged and bruised up. But once again Elden survived an accident that the police said most people wouldn't survive. If his car had caught on fire (which it didn't), Elden would have been burnt to a crisp. With no seat belt on, Elden could easily have ended up in pieces. Yet even when he crashed into the D-X oil storage building, he hit it in such a way that he was not thrown from his vehicle. One more time the Almighty God of heaven and earth looked down from heaven and answered Elden's prayers for protection.

THE PRAYER WARRIOR

For the next two months Elden was on crutches. As you recall from the previous chapter, Elden and Helen had originally planned to get married in June. Elden's auto accident, however, changed those plans. Immediately after the accident Helen moved in with her friends the McClarens to be close to Elden. Helen then came to visit Elden and his family every day. Nevertheless, rumors started going around that the couple was already doing some "hanky panky". They weren't, but these rumors made both Elden and Helen very uncomfortable. Elden prayed about their whole situation and felt that they should move their wedding day up to February 12th, 1966. Helen agreed.

Elden then talked to his pastor about getting married. He recalls that his pastor asked him what he would do if he and Helen were the only people on a deserted island. Elden replied that he would build a house before he did anything else. His pastor then told him that he would have no problem marrying the two of them since Elden's head was in the right place.

Elden was still on crutches on his wedding day. He walked into the sanctuary on crutches and leaned on his crutches as he watched his bride walk down the aisle. Of course, the joke at the time was that Helen kicked him in the leg so that he would say "I do."

Elden and Helen's wedding ceremony was a simple ceremony in Elden's home church. The pastor gave a brief message about marriage and then there were the usual vows with all that "for better or for worse" stuff. Finally, Elden and Helen kissed and were pronounced man and wife. The Lord had answered Elden's prayer to find a wife.

Both the newlyweds and their families being quite poor, there was no special reception after their wedding. The Watkins family simply took everybody out to eat afterwards. Helen and Elden were too poor to even go on a honeymoon. After the wedding ceremony and the meal were over with, they just went home to the place they had rented in Stewartsville and began their new life together.

CHAPTER TWELVE

SEARCHING FOR THE TRUTH

When Elden Shisler got married, he was still recovering from his auto accident where he failed to negotiate the curve in the road. For the remainder of 1966 and the first three months of 1967 he and Helen lived in Helen's home town of Stewartsville. However, Elden needed physical rehabilitation for his shattered knee. The nearest place that he could get the necessary therapy was in Kansas City, Missouri — almost 100 miles away from Stewartsville. So for the next three months Elden went to Kansas City on a bus every Sunday evening, stayed all week with his fellow church member John Westfall while going to physical therapy every day, and then took the bus back to Stewartsville every Friday evening. During this time period the Shislers conceived their first child. But having a child on the way caused them to reconsider whether Stewartsville provided enough opportunity for Elden to make a decent living for his family.

Merla Ann Shisler was born January 23rd, 1967 in St. Joseph, Missouri. However, before she was even born, Elden had dedicated her to the Lord. Elden had also prayed that his child would be born normal and in good health and she was. The truth is that Elden dedicated all his children to the

Lord before they were born; moreover, he prayed that all his children would be born normal and in good health and they were. There was a scare with one of them, but that is a story for another chapter.

After Merla Ann's birth Elden began praying for a job in Kansas City; then he went looking for a job in the big city. In March Elden found a job at a sheet metal shop where he was trained in sheet metal work. For a few weeks he commuted to Kansas City and stayed there during the week while working at his new job at the sheet metal shop. Of course, once Elden found a job in Kansas City, the Shislers immediately looked for an apartment there. With the help of a friend they soon found a small apartment and moved to Kansas City.

But something more profound than a physical move was going on in Elden's life. Around the time that Alfred Eugene was dying, Elden began praying that he would know the truth of the Scriptures. After his father passed away, Elden found himself praying this prayer more often. In accordance with the words of our Savior, Elden prayed that he would know the truth and that the truth would set him free. (See John 8:31-32.) Elden prayed that he would know the truth no matter what it would cost him!

In 1965 Elden began to see truths in the Bible that weren't taught in the Seventh Day Church of God. After he and Helen were married and had moved to Kansas City, the Scriptures really started opening up to him. First, he saw that there were still supposed to be apostles and prophets today and that the church should operate in apostolic order. Then he saw that the gifts of the Holy Spirit such as speaking in tongues and prophesying should still be operating in the church today. Right after that he became convinced that divine healings should also be taking place in the church in our day and age. But these truths were neither taught nor confessed in the Seventh Day Church of God. Elden discussed what he was seeing with a few of his closest friends in the church, but even if they agreed with him that these truths were important, they didn't have the same concern that these things should be occurring in the church today as Elden did.

One thing that helped Elden throughout his search was that his wife Helen had been raised in an Assembly of God church where the truths of the gifts of the Holy Spirit and divine healing had been taught as part of the Lord's plan for His church today. The Assembly of God did not teach that there were apostles and prophets today, but still there was enough in what Helen had been taught that she was very supportive of her husband in his search for the truth. So Elden took heart that the truths he was seeing in the Bible were indeed the Lord's truths even if most of the people he knew at the time were not seeing what he was seeing.

About three months after Elden and Helen moved to Kansas City, the apartment above the Seventh Day Church of God sanctuary was vacated by the people who had been living there. By then the pastor knew that Elden and Helen wanted a bigger place to live. So he offered them the apartment over the church for $25 per month provided that Elden also mowed the lawn and took care of the property. Elden and Helen had been paying $50 per month for a smaller apartment; so this was indeed a bargain deal and an answer to their prayers at the time. The Shislers immediately moved into the apartment over the church and Elden began taking care of the church grounds and property. Of course, he still had his regular job at the sheet metal shop. For once in his life the man who had survived on odd jobs for years had more than enough to do to keep himself busy.

During the time that they lived in Kansas City Elden and Helen faithfully attended the Seventh Day Church of God there. As Pastor Garland Brunson got to know Elden and saw his sincerity, he became more open to Elden's search of the Scriptures. Although he never confessed to any of the truths that Elden was seeing, he still encouraged Elden to continue in his search for the truth for himself. His pastor's encouragement was a tremendous boon to Elden. He then prayed that the truths he was seeing in the Bible would become a reality in his life and in the life of the church. During this same time period Elden felt the Almighty speak to his heart one day and say, "Come out from among them and be ye separate." (See II Corinthians 6:17) Elden wasn't sure what that meant at the time; he just knew that it was God speaking to his heart. So he prayed that he would be able to come out from among them and be separate whatever that meant.

In the late 1960's the Lord was also speaking to another member of the Seventh Day Church of God— Terrill Littrell, pastor of the Seventh Day Church of God in El Dorado Springs, Missouri. Like Elden, Pastor Terrill was searching for the truth of the Scriptures. He had concluded that the baptism in the Holy Spirit and speaking in tongues were for the church today. Moreover, he had gone on to receive the baptism in the Holy Spirit and speak in tongues himself. Like Elden he also had come to believe that all the gifts of the Holy Spirit and divine healing were for the church in our day and age.

Terrill Littrell knew of Elden Shisler, but Elden did not know of him. One night the Holy Spirit spoke to Terrill to go to Kansas City and look up Elden. At that time Elden and Helen were living in the apartment above the Seventh Day Church of God that they attended. The day that Terrill Littrell arrived in Kansas City it was already evening. When he got to the church, both the entrances to the church and to the apartment were already locked up for the night. He hollered up at Elden's apartment, but no one heard him as the windows were already closed. Finally, he found a basement window that was left unlocked and was able to crawl into the building through the unlocked window. When he got upstairs to Elden's apartment and introduced himself, Elden invited him in right away.

As they talked and became acquainted, Terrill shared with Elden how God had spoken to him to go to Kansas City and ask Elden to become his assistant pastor in El Dorado Springs. He then asked Elden, "Do you think your church is dead?" Elden countered, "What do you mean?" Terrill then expressed his belief that if the members of a church didn't have the baptism in the Holy Spirit and function in the gifts of the Holy Spirit, they were spiritually dead. Elden immediately realized that what Terrill was saying was what God had been speaking to him about for some time. He then decided that he and his family would move to El Dorado Springs in Southwest Missouri as soon as possible.

Not long after his visit to Kansas City, Terrill wrote to Elden about a house that had become available for rent in Nevada, Missouri not far from El Dorado Springs. The Shislers could rent the house for only $50 per month. In addition, Pastor Terrill also told Elden where he could get a job as a trash hauler when he moved there. Not long afterwards Elden and Helen moved to Nevada, Missouri and Elden got the job hauling trash. He then commenced working with Terrill Littrell in the Seventh Day Church of God in El Dorado Springs.

Soon after moving to the house in Nevada, Missouri in mid-1969, Elden was sitting in his living room chair one day relaxing and meditating upon what the Lord was doing in his life. As he meditated, he felt the presence of the Holy Spirit flowing into the room. Suddenly Elden had a vision in which he saw the room filled with gold to within three feet of the ceiling and he himself on top of the pile of gold. Then the Lord spoke to his heart that He would provide for him as long as he lived on the condition that he would be faithful and true to the Lord. I have known Elden since late 1971 and I have never known him to be in want regardless of whether he had a job or not.

While at the church in El Dorado Springs, Elden began seeking diligently for the baptism in the Holy Spirit. In his own personal prayer life he prayed regularly to receive the baptism in the Holy Spirit. In church he went forward at altar calls more than once and was prayed for with laying on of hands to receive the baptism in the Holy Spirit, yet for over a year he did not break through. Elden knew the Holy Spirit was with him, but he also knew that he had not received the baptism in the Holy Spirit.

Finally late in the summer of 1970 Elden prayed that he would yield everything to the Lord including his tongue. And he kept on praying this. Soon afterwards he went forward at an altar call and the Lord broke through to Elden's heart. Elden yielded everything to the Lord including his tongue. He was then gloriously baptized in the Holy Spirit and spoke in tongues. Elden felt that he was completely immersed in the presence of the Holy Spirit.

Not long after receiving the baptism in the Holy Spirit in 1970, Elden, Helen, and Merla Ann were invited over to a friend's house in the Seventh Day Church of God after the weekly Sabbath service. Everybody was sitting around outside visiting and talking about the work of the Holy Spirit. Elden was sitting between two teenagers Mark and Brenda (roughly ages 13 and 14). Suddenly the Holy Spirit fell on Elden and the two teenagers. For a moment Elden felt as if he was passing out, but then he came to himself and extended both his arms. When he did this, he laid one hand on Mark's head and the other hand on Brenda's head. As he laid his hands upon the teenagers, they both began speaking in tongues and praising the Lord. Neither of these teenagers had ever publicly confessed the Lord. Like Cornelius in Acts 10, they got saved and filled with the Holy Spirit at the same time.

During this same time frame Elden prayed faithfully that Christians he knew would receive the baptism in the Holy

Spirit and many did. Furthermore, he prayed that divine healings would occur in the church and more than one sick person in his church and in revival meetings he went to was healed by the power of the Lord. Elden had diligently prayed to find the truth of the Scriptures in reality. The Almighty God of heaven and earth was answering his prayers.

CHAPTER THIRTEEN

A GROWING FAMILY

By 1971 Merla Ann was already 4 years old and the Shislers' second child was on the way. Sara Ellen Shisler was born October 4th, 1971 in Nevada, Missouri. Elden and Helen would have one more child, but not until after they moved to Illinois. In the saga of Elden's life, however, we haven't reached his move to Illinois yet. So we will back up to the time after Merla Ann was born.

Elden truly loved his first daughter Merla Ann. Elden has always loved all of his children, but that first daughter had a special way of evoking her father's love. Elden spent a lot of time playing with his daughter and reading to her. She especially liked it when he would get down on the floor with her and let her ride on his back. "Giddy up!" she would command and away horsy Elden would go with his delighted daughter on his back. Merla Ann loved playing with her father and Elden loved playing with his daughter. Moreover, Elden frequently read to his daughter. He read to her from children's storybooks, but as his father had done with him when he was a small child, so he did with Merla Ann - he read to her most often from the Bible.

However, not everything was perfect in Elden's upbringing of Merla Ann. Often the ghosts of our own upbringing are very hard to escape. When Elden had misbehaved as a child, he had usually been spanked with a hickory switch. I'm not saying that I believe spankings are inappropriate discipline under certain circumstances. But when spankings are the only solution to all childish misbehavior and when they are administered too severely, then they are being used incorrectly. Spankings had been administered both too frequently and too severely on Elden when he was a child. So spankings were about all that he knew in regard to child discipline.

Of course, Elden did know that very young children couldn't be spanked. One evening when Elden and Helen lived in their first apartment in Kansas City, Merla Ann was fussed up and wouldn't stop crying. She was about one year old at the time; so she was still a baby and often a crying baby. Some of the neighbors in their apartment building had already complained to the Shislers that they needed to do more to keep their daughter quiet. Yet on this particular evening neither feeding Merla Ann nor changing her diaper nor walking her and patting her would settle her down; she just kept on crying. Finally, Elden was so unsettled by her crying that he picked her up and held his hand over her mouth to keep her from crying. But Elden's grip was a little too strong for his young daughter; the pressure of his grip bruised her right above her mouth. Elden felt terrible that he had hurt Merla Ann. Of course, the bruise healed up in about two weeks; physically Merla Ann was completely healed. Yet even for a young child the emotional scars would not heal so quickly.

Elden started spanking Merla Ann for misbehavior when she was age 2 - the same age that his father had started spanking him for misbehavior. Elden admits that he often spanked his daughter too hard. She behaved very normally for a child her age, yet Elden went on with his discipline program. Amazingly, Merla Ann grew up without any physical scars from her early upbringing. Nevertheless, all of her emotional scars may still not have healed. One of the things that amazes me the most about Elden Shisler is that the Lord has always used him and answered his prayers in spite of some of the horrible mistakes that he has made in life. By Elden's own admission his excessive discipline of Merla Ann was one of those horrible mistakes.

Before his daughter Sara was born, the Holy Spirit spoke to Elden, "Believe for a miracle!" The day Sara was born Elden rushed Helen to the hospital. When the hospital staff took Helen into the delivery room, Sara started coming out breach (feet first instead of head first). The doctor came out to the waiting room where Elden was sitting and explained to him the problem; then he added, "You better pray!" And Elden did pray; with his whole heart he prayed that Sara would be born normal. Roughly half an hour later, the doctor returned and told Elden that the baby had suddenly turned in the right direction. Sara was born normal as Elden had prayed that she would be. From the ordeal of her birth, however, Sara's right foot was turned out slightly to the right. Elden immediately prayed that God would set his daughter's foot straight. Dr. Babcock, a chiropractor in Elden's church at the time, told Elden and Helen that he believed he could set their daughter's foot back straight. Elden and Helen agreed and brought Sara to Dr. Babcock. Dr. Babcock prayed for Sara first and then he gave Sara's foot a quick turn to straighten it out. From that day on her foot was always straight. Once again God answered Elden's prayers that his children would be born normal and in good health.

One time when Merla Ann was age 4, she had a bad earache. So she came and told her daddy that her ear hurt. Elden had her sit on his lap and he began praying for her. Then Elden felt to put his index finger into her ear as he was praying for her. When he took his finger out, Merla Ann told her father that her ear was now okay and that her earache was gone.

Another time when Merla Ann was age 5, she felt like something was in her room, but she couldn't see what it was. She came running into the living room and told her parents. Elden got right up and went into her room. As he entered the room, he first felt a dampness in the room; then he felt as if a chill came all over him. Elden concluded that an evil spirit had entered the room and was trying to scare his daughter. So he stood against the evil spirit in the name of Yahshua. As soon as he did this, he felt the evil presence leave. After this Merla Ann went right to bed and fell sound asleep.

Before going onto a major turning point in Elden's life, there is one more noteworthy experience I should relate. As you recall, Elden had come to believe in divine healing; specifically, he had come to believe that divine healings should occur regularly in the church today. Moreover, by the time this experience occurred in the summer of 1971 Elden had already started using the original name of our Savior Yahshua when speaking of the Son of God. So on a Sunday in the summer of 1971 Elden and Helen went to a Pentecostal church meeting near El Dorado Springs, Missouri. As they attended their own church on Saturday, the Shislers were just visiting this Pentecostal church on Sunday.

Elden and Helen were seated near the back of the church. There was a lady in the church who had been ill for a couple of years. She asked for prayer for her illness. However, the pastor didn't pray for her at the time she made the request. At the close of the service the pastor (although he didn't know Elden) pointed him out at the back of the church and asked him to close the meeting with a prayer of praise. So Elden prayed. In the middle of his prayer he found himself praying that if there was anyone there who was sick, he or she would be healed in the name of Yahshua. When Elden and Helen returned for the evening service, the lady who had been sick for a couple of years testified that she had been healed instantly when someone prayed in the name of Yahshua.

CHAPTER FOURTEEN

YAHWEH NISSI

When Elden was a boy, he remembers his father Alfred Eugene mentioning the name of Yahweh a few times. His father told him that Yahweh was the original Hebrew name of God, but that people didn't use the name Yahweh today because Yahweh was a Hebrew word rather than an English word. For a boy in Missouri that explanation was sufficient. However, Elden did not forget that God had a name and that name was Yahweh.

When Elden moved to El Dorado Springs and became involved in the church there with Terrill Littrell, Brother Terrill used the name of Yahweh occasionally in his messages from the pulpit and in spiritual conversations with members of his congregation. Brother Terrill also used the name of Yahshua at times instead of the name of Jesus. The truth is that he primarily said God and Jesus, but his occasional use of Yahweh and Yahshua once again exposed Elden to the original Hebrew names of our heavenly Father and His Son.

When Elden was baptized in the Holy Spirit and experienced the Holy Spirit being outpoured on his heart and life, he felt the Holy Spirit speak to his heart and ask him, "What is my name?" Without pausing to think Elden replied,

"Yahweh." Then he felt the Holy Spirit continue, "And what is my Son's name?" Again without a pause to think, Elden replied, "Yahshua." From this experience Elden concluded that there must be more to the Hebrew names than he had been taught. After all, when the Holy Spirit asked him, "What is my name?", he didn't respond, "Yahweh is your Hebrew name and God is your English name."

Not long after Elden's baptism in the Holy Spirit, Brother Terrill Littrell began receiving a small Christian magazine named YAHWEH NISSI. This magazine was published by Salem Temple Church near Rock City, Illinois. Brother Terrill knew of Elden's interest in the names of Yahweh and Yahshua from Elden's experience when he received the baptism in the Holy Spirit. So Brother Terrill began passing the magazines onto Elden when he had finished with them.

Throughout 1971 Elden read YAHWEH NISSI avidly. I mean he read each edition cover to cover and sometimes two or three times through. YAHWEH NISSI was different from any Christian magazine which Elden had ever read before because it used the original Hebrew names of Yahweh and Yahshua in all the articles throughout the magazine. The magazine was written in English and all the articles were written in English except that Yahweh was used instead of God and Yahshua was used instead of Jesus. Elden was especially interested in the articles on the names of Yahweh and Yahshua. These articles discussed why believers should use these names today and gave scriptural and historical support for their arguments.

Elden was consumed by the articles on the names of Yahweh and Yahshua. He looked up all the verses given in the articles. He looked up cross references to these verses in his Bible. Further, he got out his concordance and researched numerous verses that dealt with the names of the Almighty and His Son. Eventually Elden concluded that Yahweh and Yahshua were not just Hebrew names; instead, he came to the conviction that these names are the eternal names of our heavenly Father and His Son and that we should use them all the time. He has done so ever since.

Since this is not a belief shared by most Christians, I am going to take a few paragraphs to share with you the essence of why Elden has a conviction about using the names of Yahweh and Yahshua. Please understand that this brief explanation is not an effort to persuade you to use the names of Yahweh and Yahshua. However, because this is a book about Elden Shisler's life and especially his prayer life, you will better understand both Elden and his prayer life if you comprehend something about his conviction regarding the names of Yahweh and Yahshua. The fact is that since Elden has reached this conviction, he has always prayed to Yahweh in the name of Yahshua.

In Exodus 3:13 we read: "And Moses said unto God, Behold, when I come unto the children of Israel, and shall say unto them, The God of your fathers hath sent me unto you; and they shall say to me, What is his name? What shall I say unto them?" In essence, Moses asks the Almighty, "What is your name?" The Almighty gives His answer in Exodus 3:14-15: "And God said unto Moses, I AM THAT I AM: and he said, Thus shalt thou say unto the children of Israel, I AM hath sent me unto you. And God said moreover unto Moses, Thus shalt thou say unto the children of Israel, The LORD God of your fathers, the God of Abraham, the God of Isaac, and the God of Jacob, hath sent me unto you: this is my name for ever, and this is my memorial unto all generations." Reading the English version, most people conclude that I AM is the name of the Almighty. However, the English translation obscures the real meaning brought out in the original Hebrew. The Hebrew words translated I AM THAT I AM in verse 14 are AYAH ASHER AYAH. These words literally mean I AM THAT I AM; so AYAH means I AM. The Hebrew word translated LORD in verse 15 is YAHWEH. This word literally means HE WHO IS. Please notice that both AYAH and YAHWEH derive from the Hebrew verb to be. The English translation completely obscures the relationship between these two words. When Yahweh speaks in the first person, He is I AM -AYAH. When we address Him in the second person or talk about Him in the third person, He is HE WHO IS -YAHWEH. Clearly the Israelites understood Yahweh this way because throughout the remainder of the Old Testament, they refer to Him as YAHWEH - not as AYAH. When verse 15 states, "This is my name for ever," the Israelites understood this to refer to Yahweh (translated "The LORD") in the first part of verse 15.

So Elden believes from this passage that Yahweh is the name of our heavenly Father and that we should use His name forever. He doesn't believe that the name of Yahweh is just for Jews. From Malachi 1:11 Elden believes that the name of Yahweh is to be great among the Gentiles just as it was among the Jews. "For from the rising of the sun even unto the going down of the same my name shall be great among the Gentiles; and in every place incense shall be offered unto my name, and a pure offering: for my name shall be great among the heathen, saith the LORD of hosts." (Malachi 1:11) LORD in this verse is YAHWEH. In fact, throughout the Old Testament whenever you find LORD in all capital letters, it is YAHWEH in the original Hebrew. Elden believes that since YAHWEH is the Almighty's name forever, the translators erred in translating His name with the title LORD.

As to the name of Yahshua, Elden believes that the Son came in the name of His Father. "I am come in my Father's name, and ye receive me not." (John 5:43) If Jesus came in the name of God, what is the relationship between the two names? However, if Yahshua came in the name of Yahweh, it is easy to see the Yah in both Yahweh and Yahshua. So the relationship between the Father and His Son is evident in their original Hebrew names Yahweh and Yahshua. This is the essence of why Elden uses Yahshua as well as Yahweh.

So Elden started using the names Yahweh and Yahshua. And he commenced writing to the publishers of YAHWEH NISSI. First, he asked if he could visit the church near Rock City; of course, the reply was "Yes." Then as he became aware that the people who published YAHWEH NISSI also had a Christian community, Elden wrote and asked if there was any possibility that he and his family could move to Salem Acres (the name of the Christian community) and become a part of Salem Temple Church. Since Elden was by then convinced of the names of Yahweh and Yahshua and regularly using Yahweh and Yahshua, he wanted to work with people who were also using these names in reference to the Almighty and His Son. But the reply came back that there was no space available at the time — either at Salem Acres or at the two houses that Salem Temple Church owned in Rockford, Illinois (about 30 miles away from Salem Acres).

Now Elden had prayed for years that the Lord would lead him into all the truth of His Word. Along with the baptism in the Holy Spirit, the gifts of the Holy Spirit, and apostles and prophets today, Elden firmly believed that the eternal names of Yahweh and Yahshua were an answer to this prayer. Nevertheless, Elden wanted to move to Salem Acres or at least to one of the houses Salem Temple Church owned in Rockford. So Elden prayed that space would open up at Salem Acres or at one of the houses Salem Temple Church owned in order that he and his family could move to Illinois and work with Salem Temple Church. Not long after praying this prayer, Elden wrote again to Salem Temple Church and Pastor Lester Anderson wrote back that there was now space available at the church's Court Street house in Rockford. Elden's prayer was answered; he and his family could move to the Court Street house immediately.

Around the end of November in 1971 Elden and Helen Shisler and their family packed up their belongings and made the 500 mile move from Southwest Missouri to Northern Illinois. Like Abraham when he departed out of Ur of the Chaldees, Elden left his hillbilly upbringings, his hillbilly culture, and his relatives to go to the place that he was certain Yahweh had shown him. Little did he know the troubles that awaited him. Little did he know that when he arrived in the promised land, his time on the mountain would be short before he descended into the valley. Little did he know that in that valley he would pray prayers that would positively influence the lives of hundreds of people. And little did he know that the greatest trial of his life would result in the most persistent prayer I have ever known anyone to pray! Around the 1st of December, 1971 Elden Shisler and his family arrived at Rockford, Illinois and moved into the Court Street house owned by Salem Temple Church. For 40 years Yahweh had been doing a work in Elden's prayer life. Now He was about to intensify that work!

CHAPTER FIFTEEN

THE JESUS MOVEMENT

At this point I will digress from Elden's personal story momentarily to look at the larger context of what the Lord Yahshua was doing at that time. In the late 1940's there was a move of the Almighty among the Pentecostal churches which Pentecostal church historians have primarily referred to as the Latter Rain Movement. One of the primary issues in this movement was that there were apostles and prophets in the church today. More familiar to many Americans were the faith healers such as Oral Roberts whose ministries were also birthed out of this movement.

However, this move of God never really went beyond the Pentecostal churches. The Lord Yahshua wanted the work of the Holy Spirit throughout His church — not just among a small minority of Pentecostals. So early in the 1960's He began to move among mainline Christian denominations to bring them the baptism in the Holy Spirit as He already had the Pentecostals. He started primarily with Episcopalians and Presbyterians, but eventually moved upon other denominations as well. Of course, the majority of mainline church members were either indifferent to or untouched by this outpouring of Yahweh's Spirit. Nevertheless, this move of the Almighty was so pervasive that even the secular media reported on what was happening. Thus was birthed the Charismatic Movement — Yahshua's move to bring the baptism in the Holy Spirit to His whole church.

Near the end of the 1960's enthusiastic Charismatic Christians were witnessing everywhere about Jesus. Many college campuses were greatly influenced by this move of God; in the midst of the anti-war movement and college demonstrations, thousands of collegians and other young people turned to the Lord Jesus and found personal faith in Christ. Mop-haired hippies became Jesus freaks; many mod squads became God squads. The Charismatic Movement expanded into the Jesus Movement as thousands found Jesus as the central meaning and purpose of their life.

Salem Temple Church (the church which Elden became a member of when he moved to Illinois) was an independent Pentecostal church that had only a few years before separated from a small Pentecostal movement called the Dawkins Movement. This movement was in turn an offshoot of a larger Pentecostal movement known as the Sowders Movement. From their origin in the 1910's the Sowders Movement had not wanted to divide over issues that divided other Pentecostals. But the divisive spirit that prevailed in the Pentecostal Movement at that time left them outside the larger Pentecostal denominations.

Years later a minister in the Sowders Movement named Reynold Dawkins began to preach the restoration of Israel and the return of the Jews to their Messiah. He preached this even before Israel became a nation in 1948. Eventually a number of groups within the Sowders Movement that felt this Israel emphasis was very important followed Reynold Dawkins and split off from the Sowders Movement to form the Dawkins Movement. Obviously when Israel became a sovereign nation, Reynold Dawkins' credibility grew and so did his movement.

THE PRAYER WARRIOR

Late in the 1950's the pastor of an independent Pentecostal church in the Minneapolis, Minnesota area became interested in the Dawkins Movement and the Israel message preached by Reynold Dawkins. Pastor Lester Anderson also saw the restoration of Israel and the return of the Jews to their Messiah. After visiting a few of their general meetings Lester Anderson joined the Dawkins Movement early in the 1960's. Yet only a few years after Lester Anderson joined the Dawkins Movement, Reynold Dawkins passed away. Like many movements the Dawkins Movement lost much of its driving force when its founder passed on into eternity.

Somewhere around this time some of the leaders of the Dawkins Movement asked Lester Anderson to consider moving to Rockford, Illinois to work with a small group of believers there. Pastor Anderson prayed about this and felt that moving to Rockford was what God wanted him and his small congregation to do. So Pastor Anderson and most of his small congregation left the Twin Cities and moved to Rockford, Illinois.

Not long afterwards in 1967 Lester Anderson reached the conclusion that women should cover their heads in church (based on his study of I Corinthians 11). Yet after he presented the head covering to his congregation, not all of his members agreed with his conclusion. Neither did the leaders of the Dawkins Movement agree with his conclusion about the head covering. Some leaders of the Dawkins Movement came to Rockford without Lester's knowledge and stirred up members of his congregation privately behind his back. Finally, the congregation split and Lester was again left with a small independent Pentecostal church.

Around this same time Lester and his wife Margaret became quite interested in the idea of Christian community based on their study of Acts 2. At first they bought an old three-story house in Rockford large enough to accommodate three families. The Andersons moved into the house at 1017

North Court Street along with their two youngest children teenage daughter Jackie and grade-school-age son Jerry, their son-in-law and daughter Henry and Judy Smith, and the Smith's young daughter Susan. Their other son-in-law and daughter Gary and Joan Kling purchased a house only a few blocks away in which they lived with their twin daughters Debbie and Darla. Lanny and Carol Hawes rented an apartment in the same neighborhood. Arthur Brown and his teenage daughter Margie also moved into the house at 1017 North Court Street. A few other people attended their small congregation, but the nucleus consisted of the people named in this paragraph.

In the late 1960's Salem Temple Church purchased an old Jewish synagogue at 1200 North Main Street in Rockford and thus moved their place of assembly from the west end of Rockford to the middle of town. With Pastor Anderson's continued emphasis on the restoration of Israel a formerly Jewish synagogue seemed like the perfect place for a church with their Israel message to assemble. So the members of Salem Temple Church assembled and they sought the Lord to move on His church in power. This was also a prayer that Elden Shisler was beginning to pray in Missouri. Eventually these combined prayers brought Elden together with Salem Temple Church.

By the spring of 1970 the Andersons were convinced that they should pursue their vision of Christian community in earnest. So they commenced looking for a farm where they could start a real Christian community. In the summer of 1970 they found an 80-acre farm four miles south of Rock City, Illinois which they could purchase for only $100,000. Brother Lester and his sons-in-law Henry Smith and Gary Kling all took out loans to raise the $10,000 needed for the down payment. In August of 1970 the deal was finalized; the Christian community of Salem Acres was born.

The Andersons immediately moved into the farmhouse at the farm and commenced the work of renovating the barn into an apartment building for people to occupy. Everyone at the church went out on Saturdays and helped with this work of renovation. By early 1971 enough living space had been created that more of the church members could move to the farm. Of course, with more church members then living at the farm more work could be done in renovating the barn into living quarters. Thus, the barn was transformed into an apartment building more quickly.

In the fall of 1970 a number of the church members were involved in a prayer meeting one afternoon at Salem Acres. During this prayer meeting Gary Schneider, a Christian who had recently joined Salem Temple Church, prophesied that people would come to Salem Acres from the north and the south and from the east and the west. Within two years of this prophecy people had moved to Salem Acres from northern Wisconsin, southern Florida, New Hampshire, and California. Yahweh fulfilled His prophetic word; Yahweh always fulfils His word.

In 1970 the Andersons reached the conclusion that Yahweh was the original name of our heavenly Father and Yahshua was the original name of His Son. They began using Yahweh and Yahshua immediately and taught their congregation the Hebrew names as well. A little over a year later they also reached the conclusion that Saturday was the holy day on which Christian believers should meet. So they switched the church meeting day from Sunday to Saturday and taught their congregation the Sabbath as well. While always retaining a born-again experience as the central message of the gospel of Yahshua Messiah, these doctrinal changes in effect transformed their Pentecostal church into a Hebrew Christian church.

Early in 1971 a converted hippie named Tom Kurtyka moved to Salem Acres. Tom was a true Jesus freak and knew many people in the Jesus Movement. Not long after his arrival he and Gary Schneider made a trip to Madison and Appleton, Wisconsin in which they related to Tom's friends the vision of Christian community and the reality of Christian community at Salem Acres. Within two months of this trip over ten young adults from Madison and Appleton moved to Salem Acres and became active members of Salem Temple Church. From a group of less than twenty members in 1970 Salem Temple Church grew into a church of almost one hundred members by the late 1970's. Many of the people who came were sinners who repented and gave their lives to Yahshua.

Into this Pentecostal, Hebrew Christian church now filled with charismatics and Jesus freaks, Yahweh led Elden Shisler late in 1971. As related above, Salem Temple Church had already started using the names of Yahweh and Yahshua in their worship in 1970 and changed their worship day from Sunday to Saturday in 1971. Their magazine YAHWEH NISSI was instrumental in Elden's move to the farm. Since Elden had already concluded that Yahweh was the name of the Almighty and had kept the Sabbath all his life, he definitely felt that Salem Temple Church was where Yahweh wanted him to be. So into the hotbed of faith and spiritual fervor that was then Salem Temple Church came Elden Shisler late in 1971. He has been involved in this church ever since.

CHAPTER SIXTEEN

NELSON KNITTING

After the birth of his daughter Sara in October of 1971 Elden started praying for a son. Joel was born December 1st, 1972; so you can see by Joel's birth date that Yahweh was not long in answering this prayer. In fact, Joel weighed into this life at a healthy 11 pounds and 1 ounce.

When Elden moved to Rockford, he first found a job working in a dry cleaning establishment. About one month later he got a much better job at Nelson Knitting Company working as a knitting machine fixer. Of course, Elden was an apprentice to start with, but eventually became a knitting machine fixer in his own right. This was a better job because it produced more hours and better pay than the job at the dry cleaners. In addition, the job at Nelson Knitting provided insurance benefits for Elden and his family.

While training at Nelson Knitting, Elden worked on the day shift. However, once he had completed his basic apprenticeship, he was transferred to the second shift. About two months later Elden was moved to the third shift. At Nelson Knitting the third shift was known as the graveyard shift. Needless to say, Elden felt like he was in the graveyard when he started working the third shift. He was tired a lot of the time in spite of the fact that he tended to sleep most of the day when he got home. One night at work Elden was so tired that he almost fell asleep into a knitting machine. He came to himself just in time to right himself and retain his balance.

By the time Elden was working the third shift at Nelson Knitting, it was 1973. At that point in his life Elden was basically working, eating, and sleeping during the week. On weekends he went to church on Saturdays and worked at the church property on Sundays. The problem with this lifestyle was that it left Elden very little time to spend with his wife and children. Although Elden didn't realize it at the time, this was when Helen slowly began to pull apart from him. Elden and Helen hardly ever argued, but inside Helen resentment began smoldering over both Elden's neglect of their relationship and over his treatment of their children. It is not that Elden didn't spend time playing with his children; he did spend time playing and roughhousing with them. Moreover, he spent time reading to them — especially from the Bible.

However, Elden's problems with his children came with his discipline. Elden tended both to spank his children for little misbehaviors that a timeout would have served much better for and to spank them too hard for more serious misbehaviors. Sara somehow managed to behave and avoid most of this discipline, but Merla Ann and even young Joel each received more than enough of their father's overzealous discipline. Helen didn't intervene when Elden disciplined their children, but underneath her resentment was seething and building.

Not long after Elden almost fell into the knitting machine at work, his supervisors moved him back on the day shift as a janitor. For Elden this was much safer; moreover, since it was daytime, he was considerably more awake. For the remainder of his time at Nelson Knitting Elden worked the day shift.

Two more things of note occurred while Elden worked at Nelson Knitting. At that time in his life Elden had a red beard although he had black hair. With his red beard Elden's boss at work felt that Elden looked a lot like a priest named John whom he used to know. Since Elden frequently talked about Yahshua at work and often witnessed to his coworkers, his boss started calling him "Father John." This nickname stuck and soon everybody at Nelson Knitting knew Elden as Father John.

At Nelson Knitting Elden met Alvin English and his sister Evva English. Alvin worked in the boiler room while Evva worked on one of the knitting machines. Evva didn't want to talk about Yahshua or the Bible, but Alvin did. Elden and Alvin had frequent conversations at work about Yahshua and the Bible. Eventually Elden invited Alvin to a Bible study that Salem Temple Church was having at one of their houses in Rockford. Soon afterwards Alvin and his wife Doris started attending these Bible studies. Eventually they both opened their hearts and received Yahshua as their personal Savior. Later Alvin witnessed to Evva and she became a Christian too. Elden had consistently prayed that he would be used to reach the lost. Yahshua answered his prayer in using him to reach out to Alvin English and his sister Evva. The interesting twist to this story is that a country hillbilly from Missouri was used to reach a black man who had some involvement in the "black power" movement before he found Yahshua.

Eventually work got slower and slower at Nelson Knitting. Finally, the work there got so slow that the company had to lay Elden off. But Elden's time at Nelson Knitting was definitely not spent in vain. Alvin and Doris English and Alvin's sister Evva had all found Yahshua as their personal Savior because Elden had been faithful to pray for their souls and witness to the grace of our Lord and Savior.

CHAPTER SEVENTEEN

THE DAY OF INFAMY

By 1973 Elden's marriage to Helen was definitely going downhill. Elden was still overdisciplining his children. And Helen was becoming more and more resentful towards this aspect of Elden's behavior. In 1973 one evening at the dinner table Elden felt the Holy Spirit come on him and tell him that Helen was thinking about leaving him. He shared this with his wife and her countenance changed immediately from a smile to a sulk. Helen, however, did not respond verbally; she neither acknowledged nor denied what her husband had said.

Then one day in March of 1974 Helen finally opened up verbally. She told Elden that she hated him and that she hated having his children. Elden had already felt his wife's hatred; at last it was openly acknowledged. About one week later Elden kissed Helen goodbye and told her that he loved her before heading off to his job at Nelson Knitting. He worked his usual nine-hour day and then returned home.

When Elden arrived home, he couldn't believe the scene that greeted his eyes. Coloring crayon markings covered the apartment walls. Most of the dresser drawers were removed from their dressers and clothes were scattered all over the floor. Toys and belongings were thrown all over the apartment. And Helen and the children were gone.

For about an hour Elden waited for his wife and children to return home. When they didn't come back by 7 PM, Elden commenced calling fellow church members on the phone to find out if Helen and the children were with any of them, but no one knew where they were. The next morning Elden talked to Alvin and Doris English (then his neighbors upstairs). Doris remembered seeing Helen and the children getting into a taxi. By this time Elden had discovered that Helen had taken all the money that they had in the apartment. Elden began to think that Helen may have taken their children and gone back to Missouri.

One week later Elden called Helen's parents in Missouri. He spoke with his father-in-law and asked if Helen, Merla Ann, Sara, and Joel were staying with them. His father-in-law acknowledged that they were indeed all there. Then he asked to speak to his wife, but she told her father that she didn't want to speak to Elden at all.

Three weeks later Elden called Helen's parents again and once again talked to his father-in-law. As before, Helen refused to talk to Elden. Elden told his father-in-law that he was coming to Missouri that weekend to see his wife and children and asked him to relay the message to Helen. But when Elden arrived at their house, no one was home. He finally called Helen's aunt and uncle and found out that Helen, their children, and Helen's parents had all gone to Silver Dollar City for the weekend. Elden's heart sank. He took the bus the 450 miles back to Northern Illinois without seeing his wife or children.

One day in June a letter arrived from Helen's lawyer in Missouri. The letter was Helen's motion to file for divorce. Elden was devastated again. Up to that point he had still held out some hope that his marriage could be reconciled. But it takes two people to reconcile a marriage and Helen had no interest in reconciliation. Craig Ridings (Elden's lawyer) advised him that there was virtually nothing he could do at that point to stop the divorce. Reluctantly Elden agreed to his lawyer's advice. About three months later their divorce was final.

Somewhere around this time Helen moved out from her parents' house and got her own place. When Elden learned this, he tried to find out where his wife and children were living, but none of Helen's relatives would tell him. From that time on all of Helen's communications with Elden were done through her lawyer.

In the letter that started their divorce, Helen accused Elden of cruelty to their children. In fact, this was one of her primary grounds for divorcing Elden. Because there was considerable truth in Helen's accusations, Craig Ridings advised Elden to stay out of Missouri or risk being arrested for child abuse. So in the summer of 1974 Elden decided that he could not return to Missouri anytime in the immediate future. It would be many years before he would once again set foot in the Show Me State.

For years and years of his life Elden never knew exactly where his ex-wife or children were living. The Bible states that your sin will find you out. Elden paid for his sins in overdisciplining his children seven times over. In one day he was cut off from his family. He never saw any of his children again while they were growing up. At first Elden prayed that his marriage would be reconciled. Soon afterwards he began praying that he would see his children again. Helen had hardened her heart towards Elden. They are still divorced and have never been reconciled. Moreover, Helen did everything she could to hide her whereabouts and the whereabouts of their children from Elden. So Elden started praying to see his children again. He prayed this prayer every day for years and never gave up hope.

CHAPTER EIGHTEEN

THE CREST OF THE WAVE

While 1974 was definitely one of the low ebbs of Elden's life, it was definitely not a low ebb in the life of Salem Temple Church. The church had grown by leaps and bounds and was still growing. People had gotten saved and were still getting saved. Believers had received the baptism in the Holy Spirit and were still receiving the baptism in the Holy Spirit. In addition to all of this, a number of the young people who came to Salem Acres were delivered from addictions to drugs and alcohol. Many people were delivered from evil spirits that had dominated their lives. Above all, the vast majority of the members of Salem Temple Church were leading dedicated Christian lives to the glory of their Lord and Savior Yahshua.

The truth is that while Elden was still living in Missouri, he had begun praying for an outpouring of the Holy Spirit not long after receiving the baptism in the Holy Spirit in 1970. He continued praying this prayer when he moved to Illinois and became part of Salem Temple Church. What Elden didn't realize is that he was in the Holy Spirit outpouring that he had prayed for when he became involved in Salem Temple Church. Of course, Elden was not the only believer praying for an outpouring of the Holy Spirit in the early 1970's.

Thousands of charismatic believers and Jesus freaks prayed for the outpouring of the Holy Spirit that occurred in the late 1960's and early 1970's. Elden was one of those thousands who prayed.

By 1973 the Jesus Movement was beginning to taper off. People were still getting saved, but not in the numbers that they had been previously. Moreover, believers were still getting baptized in the Holy Spirit, but not in the numbers that they had been previously. At Salem Acres, however, the move of the Holy Spirit was still strong in 1973 and 1974. In fact, it was not until 1976 or 1977 that Salem Acres finally reached the crest of the wave.

When Elden got involved in Salem Temple Church, he and the other members of the church prayed that the work would expand and that new groups would be raised up. In 1975 a Bible study was begun in Oregon, Illinois (a small town about 30 miles from Salem Acres). The following year a work was commenced in Havana, Illinois (over 200 miles to the south of Salem Acres). Yet in 1977 the Andersons shut down both of these outreach works. A few people from each work had moved to the farm; others were not interested in the level of spiritual commitment that the Andersons required of their followers.

But this discussion brings us to the Andersons and what they required of their followers. In 1971 the people involved in the church at that time decided to make a commitment to Yahshua like the early church had done in Acts 2. The scriptures for this commitment are found in Acts 2:44-45: "And all that believed were together, and had all things common; And sold their possessions and goods, and parted them to all men, as every man had need." To put it simply, in 1971 Salem Acres became a commune; it would remain a commune until 1980. Everybody put everything they had into the work and received an allowance of seven dollars a week for their personal needs. Of course, large items such as cars had to be purchased in somebody's name, but both the down payment and installment payments came out of the church's general fund.

The upside of this commitment was that a large amount of money was made available for the work of the gospel of our Lord Yahshua. The evangelistic efforts that Salem Temple Church was able to support because of the great financial commitment of its members was one of the primary reasons that the church grew so tremendously in the early 1970's. Furthermore, this level of commitment caused many people in the church to draw near to Yahshua.

Nevertheless, the downside of this commitment was greater than the upside. The control of too much money was concentrated in the hands of too few people. Basically, Lester and Margaret Anderson and their daughters Joan Kling and Judy Smith ran the money. At first, they sacrificed like everybody else and Yahweh greatly blessed this united sacrifice. But later the Andersons used some of this money to spend on their own personal needs. When they did this while still requiring others to make great sacrifices, Yahweh was not pleased. Eventually some of this hypocrisy began to come to light. Instead of repenting of their actions, the Andersons told those who protested that they were in rebellion and that they should not question Yahweh's anointed leaders. Needless to say, over time people started to leave Salem Temple Church. In the early 1970's many people came and very few left. By the mid 1970's, however, almost as many people were leaving as were coming. By the end of the decade more would leave than would come.

Of course, Elden Shisler prayed when people left that they would return. In a few cases they did, but usually they didn't. However, that didn't stop Elden from praying. Elden had found a good life at Salem Acres; he felt that he was with people who loved him and who were going on in truth. He couldn't understand why people would leave a place like

Salem Acres. But Elden was not part of the leadership group of the church nor did he learn much about the Andersons' hypocrisy from other members of the church. The exodus of people out of the church continued until the split of 1980, but that is a subject for another chapter.

Elden prayed for souls to be saved and he saw souls saved. Elden prayed for believers to receive the baptism in the Holy Spirit and he saw believers receive the baptism in the Holy Spirit. Moreover, Elden prayed for divine healings and he saw people miraculously healed on a number of occasions. Above all, Elden prayed every day for his children; he prayed daily that he would see his children again.

CHAPTER NINETEEN

THE RIDOTT SHOP

About 6 miles south of Salem Acres lies the town of Ridott, Illinois. In the 1970's it was a village of just over 200 people, but today it has shrunk to a small village of around 160 people. To be exact, Ridott is three blocks long and three blocks wide. Although you have to slow down to 30 miles per hour while driving those three blocks, Ridott is so small that if your mind is on something else while driving through, you may not recollect driving through it at all. Ridott still has its own post office and one tavern in the front of a house, but other than those enterprises it is simply one of those blink-or-you'll-miss-it residential communities where people live, but commute to work somewhere else.

In the 1970's, however, Ridott did have one small business — an enterprise which the members of Salem Temple Church dubbed the Ridott Shop. Salem Temple Church actually ran a small manufacturing business at this shop for a company out of Chicago. So after being laid off from Nelson Knitting, Elden Shisler split most of his time between mowing almost five acres of lawn at Salem Acres and working part-time at the Ridott Shop.

In the early 1970's a young man named Barry Steinman became involved in Salem Temple Church. Barry was Jewish by birth, but had given his life to Jesus before moving to Salem Acres. Possibly Lester and Margaret Anderson's strong emphasis on Israel and reaching the Jews for Messiah was a factor in Barry's decision to get involved in Salem Temple Church. Nevertheless, he did get involved and threw himself wholeheartedly into the work of the church.

Barry's father Alexander Steinman was one of the owners of the Naken Company headquartered in Chicago, Illinois. A division of the Naken Company, the Knickerbocker Case Company, was looking for a place to set up the assembly operation of the TV repair boxes that they manufactured. When Alexander Steinman told his son Barry about this, Barry suggested that Salem Temple Church had people who could take over the assembly operation if a suitable place could be found not far from Salem Acres. Not long afterwards, an old shop that hadn't been used for some time was located on Adams Street in Ridott. The Naken Company then made the decision to rent this building and move their Knickerbocker Case Company assembly operation to Ridott. Salem Temple Church agreed to supply the workers for this shop. Of course, this was a boon to the church because the shop provided ready employment for four or five of their members.

When the shop was started in Ridott, personnel from the Knickerbocker Case Company came to Ridott and trained Tom Heinzen of Salem Temple Church in all phases of their assembly operation. Not long after the shop commenced operations, Tom trained Jed Bennett, an extremely skilled craftsman with his hands, in all the operations of the shop. Between the two of them they trained everybody else who came to work in the shop. Within a year Jed took over the supervision of the assembly operation while Tom went on to other employment. When Salem Temple Church sent Elden to work in the shop after his layoff from Nelson Knitting, Jed trained Elden in all the jobs which he performed in the assembly operation.

What Jed and Elden and the others working in the Ridott Shop were manufacturing were metal TV repair boxes with wooden outer shells. The wooden outer shells of the TV repair boxes were made elsewhere, but the inner metal shells composed of aluminum and steel were assembled in the shop in Ridott. All the materials for the TV repair box assemblies, of course, were supplied by the Knickerbocker Case Company

First, the metal was cut to size for assembly into the TV repair boxes. Manual cutting machines were employed to cut the metal to size. Next the metal was shaped into trays through the use of metal bending machines. Then the bent metal pieces were pressed into position for riveting with an automatic punch press. After that the metal pieces were riveted into the boxes with a riveting machine. Finally, the steel pieces that separated the sections within the aluminum boxes were riveted into position.

Elden worked at the Ridott Shop part-time during the last part of 1974 and all of 1975. During this period of time he made a number of attempts to find other outside employment, but without any success. It was during this same time period that he began mowing the grass at Salem Acres. Of course, he used a rider mower to do this. But even with a rider mower it took some time to mow almost five acres every week. For example, mowing the vast lawn in front of the barn converted into an apartment building was about a three-hour job. So Elden mowed and as he mowed, he praised Yahweh and he prayed. He prayed for souls to be saved and souls got saved. He prayed for people in the church to be baptized in the Holy Spirit and people in the church got baptized in the Holy Spirit. He prayed for people to be healed and people got healed.

Of course, someone might ask, "Were all of Elden Shisler's prayers answered?" By no means. Some people that Elden prayed for didn't get saved; some people that he prayed for neither got baptized in the Holy Spirit nor healed.

But the number of people whose lives were transformed for the better at Salem Temple Church through Elden's prayers I'm sure was over 100. Were other people praying for these people whose lives were changed for the better? I'm certain that in almost every case a number of people were praying for those whose lives were transformed. So did Elden's prayers really make a difference? Yahshua declared, "That if two of you shall agree on earth as touching any thing that they shall ask, it shall be done for them of my Father which is in heaven." (Matthew 18:19) Yes, Elden's prayers did make a difference. Elden's prayers made a difference because he had no problem agreeing with others in prayer and taking up the burden of others through prayer. Have your prayers influence over 100 lives for the better?

After almost two years of looking for outside employment without success, Elden obviously had one area in his life where his prayers were not getting answered. At this point Lester and Margaret Anderson decided that it would be best for Elden to work in the Ridott Shop full-time. With only two brief hiatuses when he went to Salem Temple Church's work in Florida, Elden worked in the Ridott Shop full-time from 1976 until the early 1980's when the Naken Company closed the Ridott Shop and moved the TV repair box assembly operation back to a Chicago location.

During this same period of time Elden continued his mowing at the farm and also helped out in the farm's extensive gardening operations. However his primary work activity throughout this time period was working at the Ridott Shop. Sometimes work would slow down at the shop and there wouldn't be much to do. In these circumstances Jed and Elden always prayed for new work orders for the shop. Until the assembly operation was moved back to Chicago, Yahweh always answered their prayers.

Moreover, two more incidents of note in Elden's life happened during the years when he was working at the Ridott

Shop. In 1981 Elden moved back to Salem Acres from helping out with the work in Florida and then resided in a room at the church tabernacle. Life in his room at the tabernacle was good except for one thing: the tabernacle was overrun with mice. Elden tried some mousetraps, but the mice seemed to breed faster than the few which perished in the mousetraps. One day Elden prayed in faith and commanded the mice to leave. Within two days Elden didn't see any more mice in his room. From then on he never saw another mouse in his room while he lived in the room at the tabernacle.

Around the same time Elden was walking outside one day when it was raining. He was actually walking right by the wire fence on the west edge of Salem Acres when lightning struck the fence. The lightning then ran all the way down the fence line. Elden was only about four feet from the fence when this happened, but was untouched by the lightning. As has been noted previously, Elden has always prayed that he would be protected from the forces of nature. Once again Yahweh answered his prayers.

CHAPTER TWENTY

THE FLORIDIAN

In 1977 Lester and Margaret Anderson felt led to start an outreach work in west central Florida. Soon a number of the brothers and sisters from Salem Acres moved to the Tampa Bay area to help in the budding outreach work there. This grassroots effort was primarily concentrated in the Zephyrhills area north of Tampa, Florida. Within a year so many of the saints had moved to Florida that there were almost as many people in the church in Zephyrhills as there were in the church at Salem Acres.

In 1978 Brother and Sister Anderson asked Elden to come to Florida to help in the work there. So Elden moved to Zephyrhills and lived in a camper outside Terry and Barb Hoffberg's house. Since Elden didn't have a job when he got there, this humble abode was the only place that the church could provide him until he found work. Elden looked and looked, but in his brief time in the Sunshine State he never found outside employment. So he lived in the camper all of the five months that he was in Florida.

As Elden was not able to find gainful outside employment in Florida, the Andersons finally decided that he would be better off back in Illinois where he could at least do productive work in the Ridott shop. So before 1978 was over, Elden moved back to Illinois. There he returned to working in the Ridott shop and to mowing the lawn at Salem Acres.

However, Elden's 1978 excursion to Florida was not the end of his Floridian adventures. In 1980 work at the Ridott shop got so slow that there was very little to do. The Andersons again asked Elden to come to Florida to help in the work there and again he obliged them. This time, however, there was something definite for Elden to do.

One of the members of the church, Liz Cupp, had some horses she was taking care of. However, she got a very good job that took up a lot of her time. So she needed help in taking care of the horses. Having been raised on a farm, Elden had been raised taking care of horses. So Elden took care of Liz Cupp's horses, mowed some of the church members' lawns, and got paid for his labor. This was good for Elden, good for Liz Cupp, and good for all the church members whose lawns he mowed.

His second time in Florida Elden lived in a travel trailer on Lester and Margaret Anderson's property. This travel trailer was much better than the camper Elden had lived in previously because he had a lot more living space. Also Sister Anderson was around to cook for him; so I'm convinced that he ate better too.

Not a lot happened with Elden's prayer life during his time in Florida with one notable exception. During the late 1970's fire ants were becoming a major problem in Florida. Within a matter of weeks in 1980 the Andersons and Elden noticed a number of fire ant hills spring up on their property. They tried more than one poison in their efforts to get rid of the nasty varmints, but the fire ants not only survived all these efforts, but increased their number of hills. Lester and Margaret and Elden were at a loss as to how to get rid of these vicious pests.

Finally, the three of them prayed together and asked Yahweh for wisdom in how to get rid of the fire ants. They prayed about this for some time until one day when Margaret felt that Yahweh spoke to her about what to do. She felt that Yahweh told her that if they poured boiling hot water down the fire ant hills, the fire ants would be killed or leave and go elsewhere. So Lester and Elden went to pouring hot water down the fire ant hills. This drove the fire ants out of their hills, but at first they didn't have enough hot water ready to finish the ants off when they came scurrying out of their hills. So they loaded up bucket after bucket of hot water and Elden went back to the fire ant hills to finish their extermination. This time he kept pouring the scalding water on them as they attempted to escape. After a few days of boiling ants, only one fire ant hill with live ants remained. This one the ants didn't come scurrying out of; so Elden figured that these ants must have had another exit somewhere else. The remaining fire ants were no problem after "the great ant boil."

In 1980 the majority of the church members who remained at Salem Acres broke with the Andersons and the church members in Florida. Salem Temple Church had never known a split like this before; the split really shook up the church members who remained. Within months of the split most of the former church members in Illinois left Salem Acres and went elsewhere. For a while some of them had a small group in Freeport, Illinois, but eventually so many people moved away that this group was disbanded. Only a handful of people who were working with the Andersons remained at Salem Acres.

In fact, so few people remained at Salem Acres that these few could not keep up the payments on the property. While the church members in Florida were helping make the property payments on Salem Acres, the Andersons prayed about the whole situation and felt that they must return to Illinois to salvage the work at Salem Acres. Lester Anderson left Florida first and took Elden with him. On the trip back to Illinois both Lester and Elden prayed that Yahweh would keep Salem Acres and provide the means to make the property payments. Then independently of each other Lester and Elden both had the same vision in which they saw the word RESTORATION in large letters. Once each one realized that the other had experienced the same vision, they were both greatly encouraged. Although it looked like the odds were stacked against them being able to make the property payments, they returned to Salem Acres encouraged that Yahweh would somehow supply this need.

CHAPTER TWENTY-ONE

SAVING SALEM ACRES

In the spring of 1981 Lester Anderson and Elden Shisler came back from Florida to Salem Acres. Jed Bennett had returned before them. Work in the Ridott Shop had ceased for over a year, but when work orders had started coming in again, Jed had returned north and reopened the shop. Soon after his return the work orders increased to the point that Jed needed help in the shop to keep up with the workload. So Elden returned north and went back to work in the Ridott Shop.

When Salem Temple Church split in 1980, most of the people who left the church were the people still living at Salem Acres at the time. Yet within months of the split the vast majority of these people had moved away from the farm. Finally only Donna McKenzie, her four children, and John Honey (pronounced Ho-ne) remained on the 80 acres that had been home to almost 100 people only a few years before. Plus Donna McKenzie and her children were no longer part of the church. For months John Honey alone was the only person living at Salem Acres still loyal to Salem Temple Church. The remainder of the church members were then with the outreach work in Florida.

Back in 1978 the Andersons had decided to sell Salem Acres and then move the church there to Freeport or one of the neighboring towns. For over two years Salem Acres was on the market. Prospective buyers came and looked, but nobody ever made an offer. Finally the Andersons gave up and took Salem Acres off the market. In 1980, however, with the majority of Salem Temple Church's members then in Florida and Salem Acres over 1000 miles away in Illinois, keeping up the payments on the farm became a tremendous burden for the Andersons and the remaining members of Salem Temple Church.

That's why the vision that both Lester and Elden received when they were making the trip back to Illinois was so important. Up to that point the Andersons were still considering putting Salem Acres back on the market and trying to sell it again. But once both he and Elden had received the same vision, Lester concluded that the church was definitely supposed to keep Salem Acres. So he and Elden prayed that Yahweh would somehow supply the money they needed to keep up the property payments.

At this point I need to divert momentarily and tell you that many people had found the Lord as their personal Savior at Salem Acres. Many believers had been baptized in the Holy Spirit there. Moreover, many believers had been healed at Salem Acres and a number had been delivered from demonic oppression there. Of course, Elden had prayed for all of these things to happen as had many other members of Salem Temple Church in the 1970's. So Salem Acres had been a place where a large number of people had gone through life-changing experiences and then found new direction for their lives. Although these people are scattered across the United States today, most of them would tell you that their Christian life either started or took off at Salem Acres.

So the devil had really orchestrated a field day in 1980. He had managed to split Salem Temple Church and then had Salem Acres on the ropes. While the church in Florida had struggled to keep up the property payments on Salem Acres throughout the last part of 1980 and the first part of 1981, the Andersons had debated on what to do. After Lester and Elden had both received the same vision, the Andersons were finally certain that Yahweh still wanted a work at Salem Acres. But how could they keep up the payments?

By the spring of 1981 a number of the church members in Zephyrhills wanted most of the money that they gave to the church directed to the work in Florida. But even with the return of Jed Bennett and Elden Shisler to Salem Acres there weren't enough people with the church in Illinois to keep up the property payments. John Honey along with Jed and Elden were actually living at Salem Acres. Terry and Georgia Witt remained loyal to Salem Temple Church, but they were living in Freeport about 15 miles away. Moreover, Lester Anderson had to return to Florida for a time before he and Margaret could move to Illinois permanently.

I really believe that the devil thought he had Salem Acres at the point of collapse. In fact, I believe he was licking his chops that the place where so many had been taken out of his kingdom of darkness and brought into Yahweh's kingdom of light was about to go out of business. All the church members had to do was miss a couple of payments and the bank could repossess Salem Acres. But the devil hadn't counted on two nobodies named Jed Bennett and Elden Shisler.

Every weekday morning after Elden returned from Florida, he and Jed went to work in the Ridott Shop. Every morning the first thing they did at the shop was pray. They prayed that the work orders would keep coming in and that they would make enough money to cover the property payments. Twice work got so slow that they didn't know where the money would come from for the next property payment. Both times they not only prayed but also fasted that Yahweh would supply their need and the need of Salem

Acres. Both times Yahweh immediately brought in new work orders and both times Jed and Elden had just enough money to cover the property payment. I consider the faithful diligence of these two men in prayer and fasting one of the great accomplishments of their lives. Salem Acres is no longer called Salem Acres, but this great Christian work where so many found a new life would not still be in existence today if for a few months in 1981 Elden Shisler and Jed Bennett had not prayed and believed Yahweh.

After a few months Lester and Margaret Anderson returned from Florida and Terry and Georgia Witt moved back to the farm from Freeport. With others to help, the pressure of having enough money to make the property payments on Salem Acres at last came to an end.

CHAPTER TWENTY-TWO

PRAYER WARRING

In the tenth chapter of the book of Daniel we read a story that is very similar to Elden's prayer life. "In the third year of Cyrus king of Persia a thing was revealed unto Daniel, whose name was called Belteshazzar; and the thing was true, but the time appointed was long: and he understood the thing, and had understanding of the vision. In those days I Daniel was mourning three full weeks. I ate no pleasant bread, neither came flesh nor wine in my mouth, neither did I anoint myself at all, till three whole weeks were fulfilled." (Daniel 10:1-3) Then Daniel saw an angel of Yahweh in a vision and the angel spoke unto him. "And he said unto me, 0 Daniel, a man greatly beloved, understand the words that I speak unto thee, and stand upright: for unto thee am I now sent. And when he had spoken this word unto me, I stood trembling. Then he said unto me, Fear not, Daniel: for from the first day that thou didst set thine heart to understand, and to chasten thyself before thy God, thy words were heard, and I am come for thy words. But the prince of the kingdom of Persia withstood me one and twenty days: but, lo, Michael, one of the chief princes, came to help me: and I remained there with the kings of Persia. Now am I come to make thee understand what shall befall thy people in the latter days: for yet the vision is for many days." (Daniel 10:11-14)

Daniel prayed and fasted for three weeks with seemingly no answer to his prayer in sight. What he didn't know is that the prince of Persia (the demon that Satan had appointed over the nation of Persia) was opposing his prayers. Then suddenly his prayer was answered as the angel broke through the demonic resistance and spoke to him. Daniel warred in prayer against demonic spiritual forces that were opposing his prayer— forces which he could neither see nor possibly even realize that they were there. Yet he persisted in prayer! He persisted in prayer until Yahweh answered his prayer!

From the time that his wife and children left him, Elden Shisler persisted in praying for his family every day. Although his wife had divorced him, for years he prayed that he and his wife would be reconciled and his family reunited. When it became clear to Elden that Helen had no intention of ever reuniting with him, he gave up praying that they would be reconciled. To my knowledge it is one of the few prayers that Elden ever gave up on. Yet he went right on praying for his children.

Daniel prayed and fasted for three weeks until he got the answer from Yahweh that he was looking for. By 1984 Elden had been praying daily for his children for ten years and no answer was in sight. He still didn't know exactly where they were. Helen refused to contact him and made sure that none of her relatives gave Elden any information as to where she and their three children were residing. Helen's lawyer and Elden's lawyer had some contact for awhile, but eventually even that contact stopped. By 1984 Elden's children were teenagers. They had grown up without their father and didn't know their father. Yet every day Elden prayed for his children; he prayed for their welfare and their health. Moreover, he prayed for their souls and their salvation. And every day Elden prayed that he would be reunited with his children.

Without fail Elden prayed that he would find his children, yet no answer was in sight.

Without doubt demonic forces were opposing Elden's prayers. Without doubt Satan had been forced to assign more demons to resist Elden's prayers. Personally I believe that Elden had tied up thousands of demons in resisting his prayers. None of this mattered to Elden Shisler. He persisted in prayer and he never gave up! He never, ever gave up! At this point I'm not going to tell you the resolution of Elden's persistent prayer. But don't miss what I am telling you: Elden persisted faithfully in the same prayer day after day year after year and he never, ever gave up!

If you don't take anything else out of this book, make sure you take this: Prayer warriors never give up. Prayer warriors don't look at how slim the odds are of having their prayer answered or at how long they've prayed and haven't got an answer. They look at Yahweh and believe that He is going to answer their prayer. And they are not moved to give up their prayer by circumstances or the passage of time. Prayer warriors never give up! Elden Shisler is a prayer warrior; he went right on praying that he would be reunited with his children.

In 1987 Elden received a letter from Helen's new lawyer in Colorado. From this he gleaned that Helen and the children had left Missouri and moved to Colorado. While Helen and the children had been in Missouri, Elden's lawyer and Helen's Missouri lawyer had worked out an agreement in which Elden didn't have to pay child support. Partly this was because Elden didn't have gainful employment other than the time that he worked at the Ridott Shop. But in 1987 through her new lawyer Helen was again asking for child support. Eventually Elden's lawyer worked out an agreement with Helen's new lawyer for Elden to send him (Helen's new lawyer) a small amount of money each month for the Shisler's two youngest children. From this Elden not only learned that Helen and his two youngest children were in Colorado, but also that his oldest daughter Merla Ann may have moved out on her own. But, of course, he didn't know if she was in Colorado or somewhere else.

So the years passed on and Elden prayed on. He knew that his children were alive and well, but he neither knew exactly where they were nor did he have any way to contact them. Yet Elden continued to pray daily that he would be reconciled to his children. When 1990 rolled around, he was still praying this prayer every day and no answer was in sight. It had been sixteen years since Helen had left with their children, but Elden had never missed a day of praying for Merla Ann, Sara, and Joel. Demonic forces were resisting his prayers, but Elden never gave up!

CHAPTER TWENTY-THREE

SAWING OFF THE EIGHTIES

After the recovery of Salem Acres the Andersons felt that the church farm needed a new image. So in 1983 they renamed the church property Lakeview Hills. In the late 1970's a man had bought the property just to the east of Salem Acres and had built a small manmade lake on his property. He was an avid water skier and his own lake gave him his own practice ground. As his property was down the hill from Salem Acres, the church property now overlooked his manmade lake. Hence, the name Lakeview Hills derived from the simple geographical fact that the church property now overlooked a lake.

But that is only half the story of why the name of the farm was changed from Salem Acres to Lakeview Hills. Because of the enthusiasm and at times almost fanaticism of many of the farm's young adult residents back in the 1970's, Salem Acres had become a name that was not very popular with many of the people in the Stephenson County area. To put it bluntly, for many of the residents in the area Salem Acres was a name that had become synonymous with religious bigotry and fanatical evangelism. The Andersons thought a name change would at least break this negative association for people new to the area and for people who didn't know much about Salem Acres. Thus, Salem Acres was renamed Lakeview Hills.

Other than Elden's faithful prayers to save Salem Acres near the start of the decade and the splitting of the tornado related in Chapter One, Elden did not receive a lot of spectacular answers to his prayers during the 1980's. Of course, he prayed routine prayers for people in the church and for situations at Salem Acres and in time saw most of them answered. With Elden praying has never been about the spectacular; praying has always been what he has felt Yahweh has called him to do. Actually I believe Elden's simple faithfulness in prayer is why he has seen so many miraculous interventions in his life. But Elden has always continued faithful in prayer even when it didn't seem that much was happening. That would sum up the eighties after his prayers to save Salem Acres.

There are, however, two events of note in this time period. In the late 1970's a believer named Alan Richards got involved in Salem Temple Church and the work at Salem Acres. When the outreach was started in Florida, he went to Florida for a period of time and helped out in the work there. Then in the early 1980's when many of the church members returned from Florida to Illinois, Alan Richards returned also. Brother Alan had a special passion in life: he wanted to learn to fly airplanes. So he began taking flying lessons and eventually obtained his flying license. He finally completed his first solo flight and then flew frequently afterwards.

Now what does all this have to do with Elden Shisler? Elden was afraid of flying; he had never been up in an airplane in his life nor did he want to go up in one at all. Over the course of time Alan and Elden had become friends and Alan had become aware of Elden's fear of flying. A number of times before Alan went flying, he invited Elden to come along with him, but Elden always refused. Undoubtedly some people in the church were praying that Elden would overcome his fear of flying.

Then one day Alan again invited Elden to go flying with him. Somehow this day Elden felt differently than before: he mustered up the courage to say yes. So off Alan and Elden went to the airport and got into the single-engine plane that Alan did his flying in. Elden was praying all the way that Yahweh would keep them safe, that the airplane engine wouldn't fail, and that they would land safely. Soon Alan taxied the plane down the runway and then they were off. Elden continued to pray as they ascended into the air. When Elden finally looked out the window, he felt that he saw the fingers of two giant hands coming out from the underside of the plane. He felt that Yahweh was holding the plane up and then his fear of flying left him. At a later date Elden went flying with Alan again and felt no fear of flying whatsoever.

    The other eighties incident of note in Elden's life occurred in 1988. As you may recall from earlier in our story, Elden has always prayed that Yahweh would protect him and keep him from harm. Of course, by now it should also be obvious that Elden is one of those people who is accident-prone. This combination of Elden's prayers for protection and his accident-prone nature has produced more than one incident in his life where he has walked away from an accident with far less serious injuries than what should have occurred. In the workshop at Lakeview Hills there was a table saw. Like most of the men at the farm Elden had learned how to run the table saw and had actually used it a number of times. One day during the spring of 1988 Elden had a number of 1 inch by 1 inch stakes that needed to be split in half to be used as garden stakes. Most of the stakes were around 6 feet long; when split in half they would be around 3 feet long - just right for garden stakes. So Elden turned on the table saw and went to work.

    After splitting quite a few stakes successfully, Elden put another stake into the table saw. But the table saw suddenly recoiled and kicked out the stake that Elden had just put in.

So Elden put the stake back into the table saw and then went to hold it down with his left hand. As soon as he did this, the table saw recoiled again and pulled his left hand into the saw blade. The blade sliced through part of the first three fingers and the thumb of Elden's hand. Elden screamed in pain as his hand kicked back free from the table saw. The artery in his left thumb was severed and blood was gushing from the wound. Elden got out his handkerchief and wrapped it into a tourniquet around his hand to stem the flow of blood. Then he turned off the table saw and ran to get help.

Elden found Mark Vlad. They both got into Mark's car and Mark rushed him to the emergency room at Freeport Memorial Hospital. There the emergency room doctors sanitized his wounds and then sewed all of the gashes shut. Amazingly none of his fingers were severed. (The doctors felt the third finger on his left hand would have been severed if it were not for his wedding ring restraining the blade.) Elden had some pain and discomfort for a couple of days, but after that he went on to heal up with only minor nerve damage that made his hands less sensitive to hot and cold. Once again Yahweh had answered Elden's prayers to protect him from harm.

There is an old expression that there are no atheists in foxholes. But if you exercise consistent faith that Yahweh will protect you before you get in the foxhole, He will be there to protect you. That is one of the lessons we learn from Elden's life.

CHAPTER TWENTY-FOUR

MOWING ALONG

In the 1980's Ronald Reagan was president and the Cold War with the Soviet Union was reaching its climax. Third World countries were striving to get in on some of the prosperity enjoyed by Japan, Canada, the United States, and Western Europe, but were not making much progress. In the church the Jesus Movement was over and most churches were struggling just to hold their ground. All the surveys and polls told the same story: membership in Christian churches was down. For most Americans Christianity did not seem to provide the answers for their lives.

Elden was basically unaffected by all these events. He knew that Yahweh was in control of this world; so he wasn't really concerned about all the problems occurring elsewhere. And Elden had (and still has) a vital, living relationship with Yahshua. He prayed for the church at large that people would find Yahshua as their personal Savior and that backsliders would return from their backsliding. For Elden himself, however, there was never a doubt about his relationship with Yahshua or his commitment to his church.

The truth is that in a mobile society where most of us travel far and wide, Elden spent most of his time at Lakeview Hills. In fact, other than the time he spent working at the

Ridott Shop six miles away in Ridott, Elden spent almost all of his time at Lakeview Hills. What he did there more than anything else was mow the grass.

Now mowing the lawn at Lakeview Hills is not like mowing the lawn in your backyard in town. Of Lakeview Hills' 80 acres almost five acres are kept as lawn for the children to play on and for the enjoyment of all the farm's residents. Even with a riding mower you simply cannot mow five acres in one afternoon. Moreover, the acreage that is kept mowed includes an apple orchard with over twenty-five apple trees. There is no straight back and forth mowing when you have to maneuver around all those trees.

When the Ridott Shop was slowing down in the early 1980's, Elden began mowing part of the lawn at Lakeview Hills every week. As time went on and more and more people at the farm took outside employment, eventually Elden did almost all of the mowing at Lakeview Hills. This included not only cutting down most of the lawn with a Cub Cadet riding mower, but also mowing tight places and the sides of a few steep slopes with a push mower. Then on top of all that, there were a few bush areas that Elden subdued with a weed whacker.

How long did all of this take in a typical week? Elden says that he usually spent five to six hours per day Monday through Friday mowing the grass and whacking down weeds. Since Elden was to do most of the lawn maintenance at the farm for a little more than the next twenty years of his life, lawn maintenance in effect became Elden's real career in life.

But with no gainful outside employment how did Elden support himself? After the split Salem Temple Church was a small church and could not afford to pay Elden much for his labor. When the Ridott shop closed, Elden again looked for an outside job, but without success. Shortly afterwards he qualified for township assistance and had a very small income. The church bought his food as payment for his labor and charged him a minimal rent. Then late in the 1980's Elden qualified for SSI and in consequence had a slightly larger income. The church still bought part of his food as payment for his labor.

And what did Elden do all those hours he was riding around on that Cub Cadet mower? By now I'm sure you know the answer to this question. He prayed. Elden mowed and as he mowed, he prayed and praised Yahweh. What did he pray for? Primarily the same things that he had been praying for all his life. He continued praying for souls to be saved. He continued praying for believers who had not yet been baptized in the Holy Spirit to receive the gift of the Holy Spirit. He kept on praying for people he knew that were sick to be healed. Plus he prayed for any need that he knew about in the church to be met. Have all of these prayers been answered? No. Nevertheless, Yahweh has hearkened to Elden's prayers and many of his prayers have indeed been answered. In closing this chapter, we will mention just one prayer that Elden has prayed consistently most of his adult life. Elden has prayed regularly that souls everywhere would be saved. He particularly prayed this prayer often while riding around on the Cub Cadet mower. If you have been saved since 1981, Elden prayed for you. He didn't know your name, but he prayed for you when he prayed that souls everywhere would be saved. If you have been saved since 1981, stop and thank Yahweh now that he answered Elden's prayer and brought His marvelous salvation into your life.

Elden Shisler The Prayer Warrior

CHAPTER TWENTY-FIVE

ELDEN'S DAILY ROUTINE

Like most of us, Elden has a daily routine. The honest truth is that the vast majority of his days here on earth have been very routine days. The reason that it's important to bring this out is that although Elden's life has been punctuated with more than one miraculous event, most of his life has been like most of our lives — in a word, routine. But the lesson of Elden's routine is a lesson that's good for all of us for one simple reason: his daily routine has always included times of prayer.

Since his return from Florida in 1981, Elden's life has had the same daily routine with only minor variations. Even before he was doing most of the mowing at Salem Acres, Elden arose daily around 6 AM. First, he got dressed and then he had his morning devotions. This would always consist of at least praise to Yahweh, prayer for people Elden had on his heart, and the reading of one chapter of Scripture from the Bible. Then it was time for breakfast.

Breakfast is one part of Elden's daily routine that has changed over the years. Not long after he returned to Salem Acres, there were only a few people living at the farm. Among those few people were Terry and Georgia Witt, their children Matt and Jodie, and Elden's good friend Jed

Bennett. For a couple of years the Witts had Jed and Elden over for breakfast every morning. Either Georgia or Jed would cook the breakfast and then they would all sit down and eat together. Jed made excellent Swedish pancakes; so this was a frequent item in their breakfast menu. After breakfast they all had a brief devotion together. All of this took place between 6:30 and 7:30 AM. Then Terry and Georgia would leave for their jobs in town, Matt and Jodie would catch the bus to school, and Jed and Elden would go down to the Ridott Shop to go to work.

All of this occurred while Terry and Georgia were living in a very small house that had originally been a chicken coop. But with two school-age children, the Witts were extremely crowded in this residence. Finally, they moved to the farmhouse which more than doubled their living space. But this move broke the above-described breakfast routine. The Witts began having breakfast with just their own family; so Jed and Elden commenced coming over to the church kitchen in the converted barn and having their breakfast together there. This routine of Jed and Elden having breakfast together continued throughout the 1980's and into the 1990's.

While the Ridott Shop was still open, Jed and Elden always began their workday at the shop with prayer. Then when the Ridott shop closed, they continued having prayer together after breakfast at the farm. However, their prayer time at the farm involved more than just prayer: besides praying they always praised and thanked Yahweh and always read a chapter of Scripture together. This routine continued even after Jed went to work at Feico in Freeport making trophies.

Of course, after the Ridott Shop closed, Elden took over most of the mowing and lawn maintenance at Lakeview Hills. With almost five acres to keep up this was really a full-time job. As time went on, Elden worked out a routine with the mowing: he would mow the front lawn on a certain day of the week, the farmhouse lawn on another day of the week, and so on. Rain and inclement weather occasionally caused him to change his mowing routine, but basically it remained the same for years.

As related in the previous chapter, Elden consistently did one thing while riding around on the riding mower cutting down grass — he prayed. Basically Elden had an all-day prayer and praise meeting every time he mowed the grass. He prayed for souls to get saved, for Christians who hadn't yet received the baptism in the Holy Spirit to receive the baptism in the Holy Spirit, and for sick people to be healed. He prayed for the other members of Salem Temple Church that they would prosper and be in health. And he prayed for every trial and every difficult situation that arose in the church; he prayed that these trials and difficult situations would be resolved to Yahweh's glory. He did this day after day year after year while riding around on the riding mower. The apostle Paul exhorted the Ephesian church: "See then that ye walk circumspectly, not as fools, but as wise, Redeeming the time, because the days are evil." (Ephesians 5:15-16) Elden Shisler redeemed the time while mowing the grass: he prayed and countless lives have been changed because of his prayers.

But there was one prayer that still wasn't answered — his prayer to be reunited with his children. In his devotions and while riding around on that mower, Elden continued to pray that he would be reunited with his children. He mowed into the 1990's and he continued to pray this prayer into the 1990's. At times others in Salem Temple Church had prayed with Elden for his children; some of them had even prayed for his children on their own for awhile. But by the 1990's all the others had given up on this prayer. Elden stood alone in praying to be reunited with his children, yet he prayed on. It was part of his daily routine and he would not stop praying this prayer.

Before Jed went to work at Feico, he and Elden would have lunch together. But when even Jed got an outside job, Elden usually had lunch on his own. Occasionally he would have lunch with Lester and Margaret Anderson, but since they were the leaders of Salem Temple Church, they were often tied up in counseling or other church responsibilities. As Elden was not the cook that Jed was, lunch from then on was usually just a sandwich or leftovers warmed up in the microwave.

After lunch Elden would go back outside and finish whatever mowing and weed whacking he had left for the day. Occasionally he would help Brother Anderson with some project after that. Then he would shower and go to supper. For years the Andersons had a church meal every evening for the residents of Lakeview Hills. Virtually everybody came whether they worked a job in town or not. Different people would help Sister Anderson with the food preparation. Then after someone said grace, they would all sit down and eat together. In effect, this community supper was the one carryover from Salem Acres' communal days in the 1970's. Although each family and each individual now ran their own finances, this community supper continued on into the early 1990's.

Of course, supper finished with devotions. Then Elden would go home and watch TV or read a book. In the summertime he would often sit outside and just enjoy the evening air. Then somewhere around 10 to 10:30 PM Elden would call it quits for another day and go to bed. But he always did one thing first before going to bed — HE PRAYED. Elden prayed and then he went to bed.

CHAPTER TWENTY-SIX

THE MASTER CRAFTSMAN

For most of us there are certain people who have played a very important role in our lives. For about twenty years of Elden's life that person was Jed Bennett. Spiritually these two men were very much akin. They were not church leaders, yet they consistently supported their church with their prayers and their labors Physically, however, these two men were not at all alike. The contrast between Arnold Schwarzneggar and Danny DeVito in the movie "Twins" would be an apt contrast of the physical difference between Jed and Elden.

Jed Bennett was a little over 6 feet tall and weighed in the neighborhood of 400 pounds. (Nobody in Salem Temple Church really knew exactly how much Jed weighed.) He was, to put it mildly, one massive hulk of a man. Elden, in contrast, is 5 feet 7 inches tall and weighs all of 148 pounds. He is not a little shrimp, but neither does he have a large build. Jed had the strength to move a lot of things around that other people would need help with; Elden needs help moving anything of average size. There is one more thing of note in the contrast of these two men's physical description. Elden has a full head of black hair. Jed was completely bald; there was not one hair to be found anywhere on his head.

For years Jed and Elden worked together at the Ridott Shop. Then when Jed went to work at a trophy shop in Freeport and Elden went to mowing the lawn full-time at Salem Acres, they still worked together on projects at the farm some evenings and on Sundays. Actually Jed always had some craftsmanship project underway and Elden was his most frequent helper in these endeavors.

When the tabernacle of Yahweh was being constructed in the wilderness of the Sinai Peninsula, we read these words in the Bible: "And Moses said unto the children of Israel, See, The LORD hath called by name Bezaleel the son of Uri, the son of Hur, of the tribe of Judah; And he hath filled him with the spirit of God, in wisdom, in understanding, and in knowledge, and in all manner of workmanship; And to devise curious works, to work in gold, and in silver, and in brass, And in the cutting of stones, to set them, and in carving of wood, to make any manner of cunning work." (Exodus 35:30-33) Belazeel was the master craftsman of the tabernacle in the wilderness; Jed Bennett was the master craftsman of Salem Temple Church. Jed didn't have Bezaleel's ability with precious metals, but when it came to carving wood, he was a master craftsman of excellence.

What did Jed make? Jed made cabinets and chest of drawers. At Salem Temple Church if you needed a new dresser or cabinet, you had a choice: you could go shopping for one or you could have Jed custom-design one just for you. Many of the people who have lived or are still living at Lakeview Hills have a chest of drawers or dresser custom-designed by Brother Jed. Often these unique pieces of furniture were made complete with special engravings and a beautiful lacquer finish. For many who still own these handmade masterpieces they are their most prized pieces of furniture.

But, above all, Jed made one-of-a-kind clocks. Millions of Americans have the Audubon Society's bird clock, but only one or two have a bird clock personally designed and manufactured by Jed Bennett. Moreover, bird clocks were only one of many designs employed by Jed in the numerous clocks that he made. In fact, almost every clock he built had its own unique design and was thus unlike any other. That is why almost anyone I know who has a "Jed clock" wouldn't part with it at any price.

In many of the furniture items that Jed made, Elden was his helper. They never made anything together without praying over it and dedicating it to Yahweh first. Even with the items that Jed built without anyone else's help, he prayed over them and dedicated them to Yahweh first. This was true of the clocks; Jed made the clocks by himself, but he prayed over every one and dedicated it to Yahweh. So the owners of Jed's furniture pieces and clocks not only have beautifully crafted one-of-a-kind masterpieces, but also household items that many testify bring the very peace of Yahweh into their homes.

Jed and Elden were particularly active in this furniture ministry in the early 1990's. If Jed didn't have the money to build something he wanted to make, he and Elden would pray and Yahweh would always provide the finances that Jed needed. With many of the cabinets and dressers that Jed manufactured, the church member who wanted the particular item would provide the finances for the materials. More often than not, however, Jed had somebody in mind that he wanted to bless. So he and Elden would pray for the money that he needed for the materials for his next project and Yahweh would supply the need. Then Jed would build the dresser or clock or whatever he was making and one day the unsuspecting recipient would find the gift on his or her doorstep. To say that this selfless ministry of love blessed people would really be an understatement. When someone received the gift of a piece of furniture that at store prices would cost anywhere from $200 to $800, that individual was indeed blessed.

THE PRAYER WARRIOR

Our brief account of Brother Jed Bennett would not be complete without talking about his sense of humor. Jed did not have a life-of-the-party sense of humor. He was basically a very reserved person who didn't have much to say. But he did have the sense of the moment. Many times he could capture a moment with a one-liner that would split everybody's side. He was particularly adept at diffusing tense situations with jokes that would bring everybody involved back to a lighter perspective.

One example will suffice. In 1989 Salem Temple Church went through a brief period where there was considerable tension in the church. One day this tension carried over into the weekly Sabbath meeting. A few people got up and said things in the meeting that other people might take the wrong way; the tension mounted. In fact, the tension was so bad that you could almost cut the air with a knife. At that point Brother Jed got up, walked up to the podium, and stood behind the microphone. At first he just smiled at everybody and ran his left hand over his completely bald head. Then he said, "You know I think I need a haircut." Everybody in the church cracked up laughing; some people were laughing so hard that they were holding their sides. It took a good minute for the laughter to subside. When everybody got done cracking up, the tension was gone from the meeting.

Solomon declared: "A merry heart doeth good like a medicine." (Proverbs 17:22) Jed Bennett had a merry heart; almost nothing could get him down. With his merry heart Jed was indeed a medicine to many who were sad or despondent. If you couldn't be happy around Jed, you probably couldn't be happy around anyone.

Jed Bennett did have one vice in life. He liked fatty, greasy foods. He loved hamburgers — particularly McDonald's hamburgers. Of course, eating fatty, greasy foods is not a vice like smoking of drinking. However, if you weighed in the neighborhood of 400 pounds as Jed Bennett did, then you should have been avoiding these types of foods. But Jed didn't avoid them; he consumed them avidly. Throw in the fact that Jed didn't have health insurance and thus couldn't afford to go to doctors and you have a recipe for disaster.

During the Feast of Tabernacles at Salem Temple Church every year there was a one-day planned outing where everybody would go to a museum or a zoo or some other interesting place which the majority of church members had agreed upon in advance. During this outing in 1997 Brother Jed complained that he was not feeling well. When he got home from the outing, he went straight to bed. Later in the evening, however, he got up with terrible chest pain and called Pastor Mark Vlad for help. Brother Mark rushed him to the emergency room at Freeport Memorial Hospital, but it was too late. Jed had a massive blood clot in his heart. He died before the night passed. Jed Bennett was just 51 years old.

For Elden this was a tremendous loss. Jed was Elden's prayer partner for almost twenty years of his life, but although considerably younger than Elden, Jed went into eternity to meet the Lord while Elden goes on living and praying. Elden has another prayer partner now, but that is the story for another chapter.

CHAPTER TWENTY-SEVEN

THE END OF AN ERA

Throughout the saga of Elden's life repeated references have been made to Lester and Margaret Anderson, the pastor of Salem Temple Church and his wife. Although this book is primarily the story of Elden Shisler and his overcoming prayer life, it is also inevitably the saga of the church in which he has spent most of his adult life. As Lester and Margaret Anderson were the principal characters in the life of Salem Temple Church for almost 30 years and also major players in the life of Elden Shisler, there was no way that they could be left out of the amazing story that is Elden Shisler's life.

The amazing growth of Salem Temple Church and hence Salem Acres has been related earlier in this book. However, the Andersons' part in all this has not been related. Without a doubt Lester and Margaret Anderson had a vision that was beyond their means. For a church of less than 30 members to believe to purchase an 80 acre farm was at least a small miracle. Plus Pastor Anderson's heart of love was a gift of grace that naturally drew people to him. Both Lester and Margaret Anderson were given to hospitality and were great at encouraging and motivating people. Plus Lester was also a commanding preacher who could hold his audience's attention very well. Without a doubt Lester and Margaret Anderson were used of Yahweh to plant and build Salem Temple Church.

However, there was a downside to the Andersons that took its toll over time. They had a view of authority and submission that bordered on totalitarian. If you differed with their authority very much, they had numerous ways of putting the pressure on you to get you to conform to whatever way they wanted you to behave (or even believe). Margaret Anderson, in particular, was the master of backstage manipulation. She even got people in her inner circle to spy on "malcontents" not in her inner circle and then would apply the necessary pressure to get the 'malcontents" to behave as she wished. The problem with these control methods should be self-evident. While most people would outwardly do what the Andersons directed, resentments smoldered on the inside against this domineering control of their lives. Whenever these smoldering resentments reached the point where people couldn't stand their situation any longer, they would just pack up and leave the church community - usually without notice. But this was never a problem for the Andersons as long as more people were joining the church than were leaving.

You would have thought that the great split which occurred in Salem Temple Church in 1980 would have caused the Andersons to reflect upon their controlling behavior. Over half of the members of their church left, yet even this did not cause Lester and Margaret Anderson to reflect upon their domineering style of church leadership. In fact, if anything, their reaction to the split was to intensify their control over the remaining members of the assembly. From then on, although new members occasionally became involved in Salem Temple Church while other members occasionally left, Salem Temple Church never recovered to the glory years of the 1970's. For the most part the remnant who remained in the church were either relatives of the Andersons or believers who were not bothered by the Andersons' method of exerting authority. Elden Shisler was one of those members.

Considering Elden's earlier circumstances in life, Elden never had it so good as he did at Salem Acres. Whether working at the Ridott Shop or mowing the lawn at Salem Acres, Elden always had something constructive to do. Even after the farm switched from a communal to a community lifestyle, Elden always had something to eat. He never had to worry again about going hungry or not having food on his table. Moreover, because Elden was very loyal to the Andersons, they always made certain that his needs were taken care of. Since Elden so often had to pray for his daily bread before coming to Salem Acres, the fact that he now always had food to eat was indeed an answer to prayer.

As related previously, in 1983 the Andersons attempted to change the public image of Salem Acres by renaming the property Lakeview Hills. Without a change of heart attitude, however, nothing changed but the name. The neighbors still knew who these strange people were and still had their own perception of them. Just as a chameleon changing colors is still a chameleon, so the people at Lakeview Hills were still the same people. The Andersons, in particular. remained unchanged in their attitudes

With most of their former leadership having deserted them, the Anderson were back to their relatives plus Mark and Alice Vlad for leadership. In the 1980's the leadership of Salem Temple Church consisted of Lester and Margaret Anderson, their son-in-law Henry Smith and his wile Judy Smith (Lester and Margaret's daughter), their daughter Joan Kling, and Mark and Alice Vlad. Leadership like this gives exemplary meaning to the word nepotism When almost everybody is related, does anybody ever think differently? Mark and Alice Vlad alone on this leadership team were not infected with the Anderson nepotism.

What happened over time was that many of those who remained in Salem Temple Church began to see through the Anderson mode of church management As they did, they gradually lost confidence in the Andersons' leadership. But what were these people to do when they had problems and needed somebody to talk to or counsel with? What happened more frequently as time went on was that more and more of the church members went to Mark and Alice when they had problems rather than Lester and Margaret. Of course, with the Anderson methods of control in place, occasionally accusations were made against Mark and Alice of usurping the authority that rightfully belonged to Lester and Margaret. Mark and Alice, however, maintained a right spirit through all of these accusations and nothing could ever be proven against them. By the early 1990's the majority of the members of Salem Temple Church were going to Mark and Alice for pastoring. They had, in effect, become the real pastors of Salem Temple Church.

Finally, in 1993 Margaret Anderson's health started declining. In 1994 she was diagnosed with terminal cancer. As she had been diagnosed with a different type of terminal cancer over 30 years before and had then been miraculously healed after the church elders had laid their hands on her and prayed for her, Lester Anderson and the rest of Salem Temple Church prayed for a miraculous healing for Margaret. But this time no miraculous healing was forthcoming. Early in 1995 Margaret Anderson passed out of this life and into eternity. For Salem Temple Church it was the end of an era. With the great controller deceased and no longer an obstacle to those who wanted change, the forces of change would soon overtake the forces of resistance and cause Salem Temple Church to be transformed forever.

But in closing this chapter, we return to Elden. Throughout almost 25 years of working with Lester and Margaret Anderson, Elden prayed and saw his prayers answered time

THE PRAYER WARRIOR

and again. Probably one of the reasons that he saw his prayers answered repeatedly was that he didn't let the problems that existed in Salem Temple Church affect him. The devil will use turmoil to take away your prayer life; don't let him! Throughout all the turmoil in Salem Temple Church, Elden saw the majority of his prayers answered. Nevertheless, the year was then 1995 and Elden was still praying to be reconciled to his children. He had prayed this prayer every day for 21 years of his life and no answer was yet in sight!

CHAPTER TWENTY-EIGHT

IT'S IN THE BOOK

The year was 1997. Bill Clinton was in his second term of office as President of the United States. Communism had collapsed in Russia and Eastern Europe. Instead of Communists, Muslim extremists had become the major problem in this world. But none of these momentous happenings were major concerns for Elden Shisler. Elden had a number of people that he prayed for every day, but his number one prayer concern was still that Yahweh would reunite him with his children.

For some time Elden had thought about contacting the TV emcee Sally Jesse Raphael since she had been successful in helping a number of people find relatives of whom they didn't know their whereabouts. Yet somehow he didn't get around to doing this. But he never missed a day of praying to be reunited with his children. Elden never stopped believing that Yahweh would answer his prayer.

What Elden didn't know is that Yahweh was already answering his prayer. Sometime during the 1990's someone was putting together one of those genealogy books on everybody with the surname Shisler. Of course, the publishers of these genealogy books may not find everybody with a certain surname when they compile one of these books.

Nevertheless, they generally seem to do a very thorough job. The fact that someone was compiling a genealogy of everybody with the surname Shisler, however, I don't view as either an accident or a coincidence. Although I believe the compiler of this genealogy probably felt no divine inspiration in putting together a Shisler genealogy, I am convinced that the Almighty influenced the genealogist to do a genealogy of Shislers at that particular time.

In June of 1997 Elden received a letter in the mail notifying him about this Shisler genealogy. The letter informed him that he was listed in the book and told him how he could order his own copy. Elden discussed this letter with pastor Mark who encouraged him to order the book. So late in June of 1997 Elden sent off his order for this Shisler genealogy.

About three weeks later Elden received his copy of the genealogy of the Shislers. Of course, Elden eagerly looked through his new book. In the back of the book he found a listing of everybody the publisher had located with the surname of Shisler. First, he found himself with his name and address. The solicitation was true; he was indeed listed in the book. Then he found his ex-wife Helen and her address at the time. He had found the woman who had hidden herself from him for over 23 years of his life!

Elden looked further. He did not find entries for any of his children. So what was he to do? He had found his ex-wife, but he had written to her before when she was living with her parents and she had never replied. Whatever contact she had made with Elden had been through her lawyer. Elden thought about writing her right away, but then felt that he should discuss what he should do with Pastor Mark. Mark suggested to Elden that he pray about writing to Helen before he actually wrote to her. Specifically, he suggested that Elden not write to Helen until he felt peace from Yahweh that it was time to write. Furthermore, he proposed that Elden should consider apologizing to his ex-wife for both the way he treated her and the way he overdisciplined their children.

Elden took Pastor Mark's advice. He started praying for the right time to write to Helen and he started praying about how he should apologize in the letter. It was late in July of 1997 when Elden commenced praying these prayers. One day late in September Elden felt the strongest impression from the Holy Spirit that the time had come to write the letter to his ex-wife. He did as Pastor Mark had proposed. He apologized to Helen for how badly he had treated her and how he had overdisciplined their children; then he asked for her forgiveness. Elden included his return address in the letter. Near the end of September he mailed it.

What Elden didn't know is that one of his children (in fact, the only one old enough to remember her father) had become interested in finding her dad. Like Elden, Merla had even thought about contacting the TV emcee Sally Jesse Raphael for help in locating her father. Helen knew that her daughter was interested in finding her father. Then Elden's letter arrived in the mail. Helen did not do what she had done in the past — ignore Elden's letter. Instead, she immediately forwarded the letter to her daughter Merla. I truly believe that Yahweh put it on Helen's heart to forward Elden's letter. Since the day on which she took their children and left Rockford, she and Elden have never talked to each other. Yet Helen still had the compassion to forward Elden's letter to Merla.

CHAPTER TWENTY-NINE

PERSISTENCE PAYS OFF

Somewhere around the first of October in 1997 Merla received her father's letter forwarded to her by her mother. Of course, by 1997 Merla had grown up. In the late 1980's she had moved to the Louisville, Kentucky area, actually living across the Ohio River in Indiana first. But not long afterwards she had moved across the river to Louisville. It was in Louisville that she met Paul Moseley and fell in love. Shortly before her twenty-first birthday in 1988 she and Paul married and settled in Louisville. But this was a marriage that never worked out. Merla and Paul separated from each other in 1992 and divorced in 1993. Merla has never remarried. During her time living in the Louisville area Merla worked for the retail chain Target three times. She was employed by Target when her father's letter arrived. But the truth is that Merla had been searching for her father just as her father had been searching for her.

How did Merla feel when she read Elden's letter? In her own words, she felt like two little girls inside — one glad and one devastated. Merla had some good memories of her father, but she had even more bad memories of him. Yet she did want to know her father. So she wrote back to him immediately. Her letter literally raked Elden over the coals for how badly he had treated her as a child. She didn't spare anything in letting her father know everything that she didn't like about the way he had raised her as a child. Nevertheless, at the end of the letter Merla told her father that she loved him and hoped to see him. Yahweh had already started answering Elden's prayer. The prayer that he had prayed every day for over 23 years of his life was at last being answered!

Elden, of course, wrote back to his daughter immediately letting her know how much he loved her and how glad he was to hear from her. Then Merla called long distance information and got the phone number for Salem Temple Church. When she called the church, she had to wait a few minutes until the person who answered got Elden to the phone. But then Merla and her father talked and commenced working out the problems of the past. At that point Merla and Elden got each other's phone numbers so that they could call each other directly.

Around Thanksgiving time that year, Merla called her brother and sister at the group home where they were both living in St. Joseph, Missouri to set up a conference call between all three of them and their father. After she had both Sara and Joel on the phone, Merla initiated the momentous phone call to her father. When Elden answered, she again read him the riot act for the way he had overdisciplined Sara, Joel, and her as children. But then she forgave him. Then Sara and Joel each got on the phone in turn and each of them also forgave their father. Unlike Merla, Sara and Joel were too young to remember their father, yet they both forgave him based on what they had heard from Helen and Merla. Elden's lifetime prayer was indeed answered! He had found all his children!

Neither Sara nor Joel had telephones of their own at that time; so regular telephone contact with his two youngest children didn't commence until later. However, Elden already had Merla's phone number and the two of them started calling each other at least once a week. To say that Elden was overjoyed by this whole turn of events would be an understatement! Elden was then thanking Yahweh every day for answering his prayer.

Merla and Elden told each other right away how much they wanted to see each other. As Elden was on a fixed income, he really didn't have the money to go to Louisville to visit his daughter. Neither did Merla have enough money saved for a trip to Illinois to visit her father. But Salem Temple Church saw the need and bought Merla a round-trip flight from Louisville to Chicago and back. She arranged for a week off from Target right after Christmas to come to Illinois to visit her father. Elden was overjoyed that his daughter was coming to see him.

The last week of December in 1997 Merla took a plane from Louisville to Chicago and then a bus from Chicago to Rockford. Terry Witt drove Elden to the bus station to pick up Merla. The daughter whom he hadn't seen since age 7 returned to visit her father as a 30-year-old adult. They were elated to see each other. They hugged and then went on to have a great week together. Of course, they had to work through the problems created by Elden's overdiscipline of his daughter as a child, but they managed to do so with only minor friction. Elden sincerely repented of his past behavior toward his daughter and Merla sincerely forgave her father. For Merla there was inner healing in being able to put a lot of bad memories to rest.

In Luke 18 we read these words: "And he spake a parable unto them to this end, that men ought always to pray, and not to faint; Saying, 'There was in a city a judge, which feared not God, neither regarded man: And there was a widow in that city; and she came unto him, saying, Avenge me of mine adversary. And he would not for a while: but afterward he said within himself, Though I fear not God, nor regard man; Yet because this widow troubleth me, I will avenge her, lest

THE PRAYER WARRIOR

by her continual coming she weary me.' And the Lord said, 'Hear what the unjust judge saith. And shall not God avenge his own elect, which cry day and night unto him, though he bear long with them? I tell you that he will avenge them speedily. Nevertheless when the Son of man cometh, shall he find faith on the earth?'" (Luke 18:1-8) This parable sums up the story of Elden's persistent prayer. In essence, Yahweh is telling us: "Come wear Me out and see if I won't answer your prayer." The problem with most of us is that we don't take Yahweh seriously enough when it comes to any difficult prayer that isn't answered right away. Most of us just give up. But Elden Shisler never gave up! Why Yahweh didn't answer Elden's prayer for over 23 years I don't know. What I do know is that in the end He answered it!

If the Lord were physically here on the earth today talking to His disciples, He wouldn't need the parable of the unjust judge. He could just tell the story of Elden's persistent prayer!

CHAPTER THIRTY

NEW BEGINNINGS CHURCH

After Margaret Anderson passed away in 1995, Salem Temple Church entered into a period of momentous changes. Lester Anderson was a wonderful preacher, yet he was never the controller that his wife was. As Mark Vlad had already been doing the majority of the pastoring of the members of Salem Temple Church, Lester Anderson let him continue to do so. By 1997 virtually everybody in the congregation recognized that Mark had in effect become the real pastor of Salem Temple Church. Lester recognized this too.

In 1997 Mark Vlad and a number of the other members of the congregation got Lester Anderson's agreement to change the constitution of Salem Temple Church. This was the first step in a radical transformation of this assembly. The new constitution did away with the autocratic rule of one man. Instead, Pastor Mark sought the advice of the whole assembly in leading Salem Temple Church. Specifically, the new constitution created a board of trustees to oversee the church property of Lakeview Hills. The board would consist of five trustees elected by the members of the congregation. The new constitution also required the church to hold an annual meeting in which all the members of the congregation could air their opinions and vote for the trustee positions that were up for re-election. In addition, the constitution created a three-person finance committee to run the finances of Salem Temple Church.

Shortly after the ratification of the new church constitution Lester Anderson decided to retire completely. He moved away from Northern Illinois to live with one of his children in another state. Although he has been back to visit a number of times, he has never again resided at Lakeview Hills. Not long after Brother Anderson moved away, his daughter Judy Smith and her husband Henry also decided to move away to be near one of their children. The church that had once been controlled by Lester and Margaret Anderson and the members of their family no longer had one Anderson family member in it. For Salem Temple Church this was indeed a new day.

In 1998 and 1999 Pastor Mark began attending seminars at Willow Creek Church in northwest suburban Chicago. His natural brother Mike Vlad, a pastor in the Seventh Day Church of God, had already attended seminars at Willow Creek and had shared with Mark how much he had benefited from them. So Pastor Mark went to a seminar with Mike and got so much out of it that he started going to Willow Creek seminars on his own. Under Lester Anderson's leadership Salem Temple Church had become a fortress unto itself. The Andersons felt that they had the divine inspiration from Yahweh and consequently felt no need to get any inspiration from anybody else. Mark Vlad, in contrast, felt that he should be able to learn from any other brother or sister in Messiah. Pastor Mark's attendance at Willow Creek seminars was a radical departure from the Salem Temple Church of the past.

At these seminars Brother Mark learned a number of truths which he brought back to his congregation. Two of these truths in particular stand out: a burden for lost souls and an emphasis on service in the church. I cannot tell you how many messages Mark has preached on these two subjects since 1999; I can tell you that he has ministered on these subjects repeatedly. He has just continued talking about reaching lost souls and serving the church until his congregation has changed and commenced incorporating these truths into their lives. To go from a fortress mentality to a reach-the-world mentally has indeed been no easy task.

With all of these changes going on in the congregation, by 1999 most of the members of Salem Temple Church had become uncomfortable with the name of their assembly. The word "Salem" means peace; so it is not a bad word in itself. However, the word "Salem" is associated in America with the Salem witch trials in colonial Massachusetts. In addition, virtually all the members of the assembly wanted to clear the association this name had for them with the intolerance of the Anderson era in the church. So the push was on to rename Salem Temple Church.

In 2000 two meetings were held to rename Salem Temple Church. In the first meeting a number of possible new names for the church were put forward and then voted upon until the list was reduced to five possible new names. A week later a second meeting was held and the five remaining possible new names were voted upon; the ballot went to the new name New Beginnings Church.

And what was Elden doing during all these momentous changes? Elden had always been happy with the Andersons when they ran Salem Temple Church, yet he had always gotten along well with Mark and Alice Vlad too. Elden didn't especially pray for these changes, but he didn't oppose them either. While these changes were taking place, Elden primarily prayed that the will of Yahweh would be done. That is what most of the church prayed and the members of New Beginnings Church believe that Yahweh answered their prayer.

Besides, Elden had found his children and was already rebuilding a relationship with his daughter Merla. Yet he continued to pray that he would have a relationship with his other two children as well.

CHAPTER THIRTY-ONE

LIKE TWO PEAS IN A POD

Since Merla came to visit her father late in 1997, Elden and Merla have been communicating regularly. They call each other on the phone several times each week and have great conversations. Moreover, they often pray together over the phone during these conversations.

In the fall of 1998 Sara wrote her father after getting her father's address from Merla. Of course, Elden wrote back immediately. Since Sara had neither a telephone of her own nor access to one then, corresponding by letters was the only method of communication available to both father and daughter at that particular time. Elden has never owned a computer; he has never used the Internet and doesn't know how to use it So communication by e-mail wasn't really an option between Sara and Elden. Nevertheless, they corresponded regularly until Sara moved to where she had access to a telephone.

Now Elden never just prayed that he would find his children. Of course, he prayed over and over that he would find them. But he also prayed that his children would find Yahshua as their personal Savior. For Elden this meant that his children would repent of their sins and give their lives to Yahshua as both Lord and Savior. Yahweh answered this prayer before

Elden ever found his children. Merla, Sara, and Joel have all repented of their sins and invited Jesus into their lives as their Lord and Savior. Elden also prayed that all his children would receive the baptism in the Holy Spirit; Yahweh answered this prayer as well. But with Sara the Almighty threw in something extra; Yahweh poured His joy into Sara beyond anything Elden ever prayed or imagined. In Ephesians 3:20 the apostle Paul encourages us: "Now unto him that is able to do exceeding abundantly above all that we ask or think, according to the power that worketh in us." Yahweh gave Sara His joy beyond anything Elden ever prayed.

So Sara and Elden started corresponding on a regular basis in 1998. Then in 1999 Sara moved to a group home where she had access to a telephone. However, she could not make outgoing long distance calls except in an emergency. But Elden could now call his daughter. So Elden began calling Sara once a week and has continued doing so ever since. Needless to say, father and daughter have plenty to talk about since they have one great thing in common — their love for our Savior. Elden frequently encourages his daughter over the phone and they often pray together over the phone. Sara encourages her father in these conversations as well. Of course, these conversations didn't go on very long before Elden and Sara wanted to see each other.

In June of 2000 Sara finally saved up enough money to take the bus from Western Missouri to Northern Illinois to see her father. As you recall, Elden never had a career job; so he never had much money. Quite simply, he didn't have the money to purchase a bus ticket to go visit his daughter. But both Elden and Sara were praying that they would see each other in person. Yahweh answered their prayers by allowing Sara to save enough money to take the bus to visit her father. I need to add here that neither Elden nor Sara drive; so one of them driving a car to visit the other was not an option. (Although Elden did drive when he was younger, he stopped driving in his early 40's because of his penchant for getting into auto accidents.)

In June of 2000 Terry Witt drove Elden to the bus station in Rockford, Illinois to pick up Sara. Both father and daughter were overjoyed to see each other. Elden lives in a small bungalow at Lakeview Hills. But although his bungalow only has a living room, kitchen, one bedroom, and a small bathroom, Elden bunked out on a cot in the living room during the time that Sara was visiting him so that she could sleep in the bedroom. Sara visited Elden for almost three weeks and what a time they had together! They prayed together, read and studied the Bible together, talked together, walked together, fellowshipped with other believers at Lakeview Hills together, and even swung on the two-seat swing in the front yard together. When someone saw them swinging on the swing together, she proclaimed that they were like two peas in a pod. The expression stuck. Sara and Elden are like two peas in a pod in more ways than one. In essence, they're soul mates. They both love to pray, love to read the Bible, and love to go to church. They think in similar veins and even some of their mannerisms are the same. They may have been separated by time and space for over 25 years of their lives, but that didn't prevent Yahweh from working a miracle of unity between them.

When Sara finally left to go back home to Missouri, it was a difficult day for Elden as I'm sure that it was for Sara. But for the many of us who had grown to love and appreciate Sara during her brief visit, there was also a sense of separation. Elden loves all three of his children, but the special relationship that he and Sara developed during June and July of 2000 continues to this day.

In both 1998 and 1999 Terry and Georgia Witt went to visit their son Matt in Georgia for the Thanksgiving holiday weekend. Both times they took Elden along, dropped him off in Louisville to see Merla for the weekend, and then brought him back home on their return trip from Georgia. On both occasions Elden had wonderful visits with his daughter. Then in 2000, Michael Banak, a fellow believer from the Chicago suburbs, took Elden to Louisville at Thanksgiving to visit Merla. Once again Elden and his daughter had a wonderful time.

These Thanksgiving visits speak volumes about Elden's prayer life. The truth is that Elden's whole life has been a thanksgiving session with Yahweh. Elden thanks Yahweh every day for restoring his children to him. Moreover, he thanks Yahweh repeatedly for saving his soul and baptizing him in the Holy Spirit. Plus he thanks Yahweh often for his church and all the other believers that Yahweh has saved with him. With Elden prayer is never just asking. Elden always starts praying by giving thanks first. He praises Yahweh and thanks Him for all His blessings, usually listing one or two of these blessings specifically. Then he makes his requests. Most of us have been given more natural endowments than Elden Shisler ever had. But with his limited natural endowments Elden has always been thankful for everything that Yahweh has done for him. I truly believe that this is one of the reasons that he has been so successful in prayer.

CHAPTER THIRTY-TWO

WHERE TWO OR THREE

In Matthew 18:19-20 we find recorded these words of our Lord Yahshua: "Again I say unto you, That if two of you shall agree on earth as touching any thing that they shall ask, it shall be done for them of my Father which is in heaven. For where two or three are gathered together in my name, there am I in the midst of them." Throughout this book I have recorded Elden's participation in prayer with other believers. Elden has never taken the attitude that I'm so good at prayer that I don't need to pray with other people. On the contrary, Elden has always been willing to pray with other believers. The words of Yahshua quoted above clearly indicate that we are more effective in prayer if we can agree with others in prayer. Elden is a living role model of this behavior.

For almost twenty years of his life Elden's prayer partner was Jed Bennett. Their agreement in prayer and their willingness to sacrifice saved Salem Acres from foreclosure. Plus many of the other things which they agreed upon in prayer have been related earlier in this book. Both men were more effective in prayer together than either one of them would have been alone because of their consistent agreement in prayer. But as related previously, Jed Bennett passed out of this life and into eternity in 1997. Elden needed a new prayer partner.

The truth is that Elden prayed with others even while Jed was alive. One person with whom he prayed regularly for years was Terry Witt. Every Sunday morning at 7:30 AM they would meet together for prayer and focus on the needs of the physical property of Lakeview Hills. What sort of things did they pray for? Elden and Terry prayed for new equipment that the farm needed. They prayed that equipment that wasn't working perfectly would continue working. Furthermore, they prayed for supplies that were needed around the farm. And they prayed that Yahweh would supply the funds for all these needs.

As time passed, Terry and Elden saw their requests answered. So they kept praying their equipment and supplies prayers and Yahweh kept answering their requests. Did they save any money to help bring some of their prayers to pass? Yes, they did. But more often than not, their prayers were answered through somebody giving Lakeview Hills a piece of equipment or somebody at the farm finding a good used piece of equipment at a bargain price. The moral here is that we can even pray about things which we usually take for granted.

Jed and Elden had prayed together almost every day. Terry and Elden, however, only prayed together once a week. Elden still desired a prayer partner with whom he could pray more than once a week. Jed died in 1997; in the summer of 1998 Yahweh answered Elden's prayer for a new prayer partner. I have become the answer to this prayer.

In May of 1998 Emily and I moved to Lakeview Hills. Having lived at Salem Acres in the early 1970's when the church ran the property as a commune, it was quite refreshing to see that the former commune had become in every respect a community. To put it simply, the residents of Lakeview Hills today lead their own lives without the totalitarian authority structure of the past. Many of the members of New Beginnings Church don't even live at the farm. Most of them live in Freeport and come out to the church for meetings only. Those few of us who do live at Lakeview Hills work on a few projects together on weekends, but otherwise we lead our lives like most Christians in America: we go out to work, we come home and spend time with our families, we have our recreation times on weekends, and we attend our weekly church meetings.

When I returned to Lakeview Hills, Yahweh had been dealing with me for some time about my prayer life. To put it simply, I knew that I needed to pray more. One day I was sharing this with Elden and he responded that he would always be willing to pray with me. So we started praying together. At first we met together two evenings a week for prayer, but not long after we commenced praying together, we increased our joint prayer time to three evenings a week. For almost a year Ron Dillman joined us in these prayer meetings. Then when Ron got quite busy with a number of projects at Lakeview Hills, it was just Elden and I praying together again. There was a period when I became so busy at my job that we reduced our prayer meetings to one evening per week. However, it wasn't long until we returned to praying together twice every week.

Then early in 2002 I accepted a promotion to sales manager with the insurance company I work for. With that job I traveled considerably and often didn't get home till late. In these circumstances for about eight months Elden and I didn't meet together regularly for prayer. Occasionally we got together on a Sunday morning and prayed, but we had no set prayer times as before. Then in October of 2002 I resigned my position as a sales manger and went back as an agent. However, the only sales route available at the time was over an hour's drive from my home. Yet even in this situation I wasn't driving quite as much as I was as a sales manager. So Elden and I went back to meeting for prayer once a week. In March of 2003 I switched to a sales route that was much closer to where I live. Not long afterward Elden and I returned to meeting for prayer twice a week. We have continued praying together twice weekly ever since.

So what have we prayed for? Furthermore, have all our prayers been answered? I will tell you up front that not all of our prayers have been answered. For example, during the first year that we prayed together, we prayed for three teenagers in our church that were not making it spiritually. In the end all three of them dropped out of the church; not one of them is leading a Christian life today But these former teenagers are only in their 20's now; so Yahweh has plenty of time to answer our prayers by bringing them to a born-again experience and living faith in Yahshua. The great English Christian George Mueller prayed every day that certain people whom he knew would find Jesus as their personal Savior. When he died, two of these people still weren't saved; the doubters were quick to point out that not all of George's prayers were answered. But within ten years of his death these last two had found Christ like the others for whom George Mueller had prayed.

When Merla still lived in Louisville, she asked her father to pray for a friend of hers who was quite ill. The illness he had was something that people recover from gradually over time. So Elden brought this request to our prayer meeting and we agreed in faith that Merla's friend would be healed. When Elden talked to Merla on the phone the following week, he found out that her friend had suddenly recovered and had no vestiges of his former illness A recovery that should have taken months took a week. Yahweh's answer to this request exceeded all our expectations.

At Lakeview Hills we used to have some renters who weren't members of New Beginnings Church. (Actually we still have one family renting on our property who are not church members.) We really don't have any problem with renters so long as they pay their rent. But this one family was always behind on their rent — often more than a month behind. We had compassion because they had some job problems, but even when their job situation improved, their rent payment habits improved only marginally. Then suddenly the wife took some interest in the church and began attending church meetings. Not long afterwards a friend of hers also attended some church meetings with her. Since this friend was also looking for a place to rent, the church agreed to rent her a trailer at Lakeview Hills. No more had she moved into the trailer than both women abruptly stopped attending church meetings. Then the first couple's rent payment habits once again deteriorated. On top of that the new renter paid late from the start.

Although Elden and I were never directly involved in dealing with renters at Lakeview Hills, we did become aware of the problem that the church was having with these renters. At first we prayed that they would get saved and give their hearts to Yahshua as their personal Savior. Moreover, we prayed that they would improve their rent payment habits and catch up on what they owed. Yet over time their attitudes deteriorated and their rent payment habits got even worse. Finally, we prayed that Yahweh would either change their hearts and let them find Yahshua or cause them to leave and move elsewhere. We prayed that prayer about three months. One day we discovered that both renters had abruptly moved out the day before. We would have rather that they had given their hearts to the Lord, but Yahweh did answer our prayer.

In some cases Elden and I have prayed for people or circumstance that our whole church has been praying for. A good example of this would be Rachel Garza. Rachel is a fully committed Christian who for years worked at the medical library at Swedish American Hospital in Rockford. While there and at her previous job at Freeport Memorial

Hospital in Freeport, she was always a faithful witness to the saving grace of our Lord Yahshua. In the late 1980's she led her co-worker Adrienne Mooney to the Lord while working at Freeport Memorial Hospital. But in 1997 Rachel suffered the first of two strokes. The stroke was so damaging that she was not able to return to work. Then after the second stroke the doctors said that there was so much damage to her brain that she might not be able to speak again. Needless to say, from the time of her first stroke all the members of New Beginnings Church have prayed for the healing of this beloved fellow member. Of course, Elden and I have also prayed for her healing frequently in our prayer time. At this point Rachel has not been healed. Nevertheless, she has recovered far beyond anything her doctors ever expected. Particularly, she is speaking and speaking well. Although the strokes have damaged her ability to process what other people are saying, nevertheless she is now able to process virtually anything somebody else is saying to her if whoever is speaking to her just speaks a little more slowly than usual. All of this has astounded her doctors since they consider the areas of her brain that control these functions damaged beyond recovery.

Late in 2005 Ron Deen began joining Elden and I for prayer. Moreover, since October of last year New Beginnings Church has had a weekly prayer meeting every Wednesday night. Elden prayed for years that more people in this church would get a burden to pray. Yahweh is now answering that prayer.

CHAPTER THIRTY-THREE

PASSING THE TORCH

One of the measures of the effectiveness of any ministry is the effect that it has on other people. Over the years Elden has definitely encouraged other people to pray. Moreover, he has always been willing to pray with other people. Both Jed Bennett and Terry Witt were men of prayer in their own right, yet I'm certain that their time praying with Elden increased their faith and the effectiveness of their prayers.

With this thought in mind let's look briefly at a few things that have happened in my own prayer life since I have been praying with Elden. Two particular incidents will suffice.

Recall that I am a life insurance salesman by occupation. In June of 2000 I went through a period where I wasn't turning up many new prospects. Finally, during the last week of June I reached the point of desperation with my insufficient prospecting. One evening I prayed a desperate prayer: "Yahweh, I need some prospects. I need referred leads. I need to run into other people who are interested in life insurance in customers' houses." And then I prayed this wild prayer: "I don't care if people hail me down on the streets! Yahweh, I need some prospects." Yahweh was listening to my prayer.

THE PRAYER WARRIOR

On Monday July 3rd I started early because I had a lot of people to see. With the next day being the 4th of July holiday I actually had more than the usual number of people to see. At about 9:30 AM I knocked on the door of a customer who worked third shift trying to catch her before she went to bed, but there was no answer. As I walked back to my car, a Freeport Park District truck with three guys in it pulled up beside me. I didn't recall seeing any of these three guys before in my life. Yet the driver queried me: "You're the insurance man, aren't you?" 'Yes, I am," I replied. "Do I know you?" "No," the driver responded, "but I've seen you around." Then he added, "I need some life insurance." So I took down his name, address, and phone number and made arrangements to call him later that week. At that point no thought of my prayer came into my mind.

At 10 AM I went to an appointment where a lady was supposed to look at life insurance, but she wasn't home. Since she was retired, I figured that she was out running some errand: so I left her a note that I would return at 11 AM. Then I went and collected premiums from a few other customers before returning to her house at 11 AM. This time she was home. So I had the interview with her and sold her a policy. As I was finishing the interview with my new customer, a Rent-A-Center truck pulled up in front of her house with some furniture that she was renting to own. Two guys got out of the truck and came up to her house. I knew the guy driving the truck, but his helper I didn't know. At this point I had to go back to my car to get something for my new customer. As I was about to go back in the house, the guy I didn't know met me and asked me what I did for a living. I replied that I sold life and health insurance. He then asked me if I also sold renters insurance and I answered in the affirmative. He then said that he needed some renters insurance. So I took down his name, address, and phone number and promised to call him the next week. I then went to thank the guy I did know for referring this new potential customer to me, but he told me that he hadn't said anything to his co-worker about what I did for a living.

When I got in my car and started to drive, it hit me: I had prayed "I don't care if people hail me down on the streets." In less than two hours on the same day two people whom I didn't know hailed me on the streets and approached me about insurance! In case you don't know this, people almost never hail an agent on the streets looking for insurance. Later I calculated that in the previous twenty-five years of selling insurance only 3 or 4 people had ever approached me on the streets looking for insurance. Figuring that I probably forgot one, let's say that previous to July 3rd, 2000 only 5 people in twenty-five years had approached me on the streets about life insurance.

Now let's take this a step further: I approach on the average 40 people each week attempting to interest them in insurance. This means that I approach around 2000 people each year. However, since only 5 people (at the most) had approached me on the streets in 25 years, that means that only one person approached me on the streets every 5 years. Specifically, that means that for every 10,000 people I approached, one person approached me on the streets. So what would be the odds of 2 people approaching me on the streets on the same day? For the answer to that question you have to multiply 10,000 by 10,000: the odds of 2 people approaching me on the streets on the same day are 1 in 100 million. Or you can take the simpler approach: Yahweh answered my wild prayer.

In March of 2003 I was working in Eastern Iowa over two hours from my home on the day before payday. At about 2 PM I bought a soft drink and then realized that I only had four dollars left in my pocket. All my credit cards had been torn up and thrown away two years before. As I only had half a tank of gasoline left in my car, I resolved that I would have to keep the four dollars for gasoline and skip supper. When

THE PRAYER WARRIOR

I drove back to the Quad Citties, I was down to one-quarter of a tank of gasoline. So I found a station with a good price and spent my last four dollars putting gasoline in my car. My gas gauge registered just under one-half of a tank. When I reached Sterling, Illinois, I was halfway home. I looked at my gas gauge: it registered just under one-quarter of a tank. From previous experience I knew that I would make it to my home a little over 50 miles away, but the yellow warning light would come on before I made it home. When the yellow warning light came on in the car I had at the time, it always made a ding sound.

So I took off from Sterling and as I did, I resolved not to look at my gas gauge until I got home. Then when I got about 20 miles from home, I started praying that the yellow warning wouldn't come on until I reached German Valley (about 11 miles from Lakeview Hills). When I made it to German Valley, I then prayed that the yellow warning light would not come on before I arrived at Highway 20 (about 7 miles from Lakeview Hills). When I reached Highway 20, I then started praying each mile that I would make it another mile without the yellow warning light coming on. I prayed this prayer continuously each mile until I arrived home. When I finally parked, I at last looked at my gas gauge. It was right on the line where the yellow warning light should have come on, but the yellow warning light did not come on. I turned the car off and thanked Yahweh for answering my prayers all the way home.

The next morning I hauled some trash out to my car to take out to the big trash bin behind the shop. The distance to be traveled was less than one-twentieth of a mile. As I drove the car to the trash bin, I heard the ding! The yellow warning light at last came on!

CHAPTER THIRTY-FOUR

ELDEN'S PRAYER PRINCIPLES

―〜―

Elden has never stated any prayer principles to me. However, from my observance of his prayer life I have elicited five prayer principles. The Bible supports every one of these rules of prayer. Since you are reading this book, hopefully one of your reasons for doing so is to make your own prayer life more effective. It is my firm conviction that the more we apply these five prayer principles, the more effective our prayer life will be.

PRAYER PRINCIPLE ONE

PRAY ABOUT ANYTHING AND EVERYTHING. Another way to state this rule of prayer is **NOTHING IS TOO UNIMPORTANT TO PRAY ABOUT.** If you want a pigeon, you pray for a pigeon. If you want a house, you pray for a house. If you want a spouse, you pray for a spouse. If you want the mice out of your house, you pray for them to leave your house. This doesn't mean that you shouldn't put out any mousetraps. But getting the mice out of your house is not too unimportant for Yahweh not to be listening to your prayer.

Some people say that Yahweh is too busy to listen to little matters that really aren't that important. The apostle John exhorts us: "And if we know that he hear us, whatsoever we ask, we know that we have the petitions that we desired of him." (I John 5:15) "Whatsoever we ask"! Yahweh is interested in whatsoever we ask. Yahshua tells us that even the hairs on our heads are all numbered (Matthew 10:30) If Yahweh has time to number all the hairs on all of our heads, then He certainly has time to listen to our prayer requests — however insignificant they may seem to us or to others. So whatever you are concerned about, pray about. **PRAY ABOUT ANYTHING AND EVERYTHING.**

PRAYER PRINCIPLE TWO

MAKE PRAYER A HABIT. Don't wait till you're in a foxhole to start praying. Don't wait until your back is against a wall to commence bringing your petitions to Yahweh. If you're in a foxhole or your back is against a wall, you need to pray. But don't wait until you're in a difficult situation to begin praying. The time to start praying is now. Then continue praying tomorrow and the next day and the day after that. If you miss a day, begin again the next day. Prayer won't become a habit until you make it a habit. And it takes time to turn any behavior into a habit.

Did Elden Shisler miss praying some days when he first started praying? Yes, he did. Elden missed praying a lot of days when he commenced praying. Nevertheless, he kept at it and eventually he formed the habit of praying every day. As time went on, he expanded this habit into praying more than once every day. The apostle Paul exhorts us: "Pray without ceasing." (I Thessalonians 5:17) Now I don't believe that this means we are to be consciously praying every second. However, I do believe this means that we should pray every day.

Now I am certain that some people who are reading this are saying: "I've tried daily devotions before and I've never been able to keep them going." Some of you may have even tried numerous times to keep daily devotions going, but without any lasting success. If this is any consolation to you, I tried to keep daily devotions going most of my life, but had no success until the last five years. What made the difference in the last five years? Before I started daily prayer this time, I first prayed earnestly that Yahweh would give me both the grace and the will power to keep devotions going. The devil fights daily prayer so ferociously that we need the help of the Almighty to sustain any regular prayer life.

If someone were to ask me the main reason why Elden Shisler has been so successful in prayer, I would answer because he made prayer the daily habit of his life. **MAKE PRAYER A HABIT.**

PRAYER PRINCIPLE THREE

START PRAYER WITH THANKSGIVING. As I mentioned before, I have never prayed with Elden where he hasn't praised and thanked Yahweh prior to making any requests. Elden always commences prayer by worshipping Yahweh and thanking Him for all of His goodness and mercy to His people. He usually thanks Him for some specific answers to prayer as well. Only after thanking Yahweh does Elden began bringing his petitions before Yahweh. We may live in one of the most unthankful generations in the history of this planet, but that doesn't mean that we should neglect to give thanks.

Someone may object: "I haven't had any answers to prayer; so I don't know what to thank the Almighty for." The essence of your dilemma is in your thinking that you don't know what to thank Yahweh for without a specific answer to prayer. Thank the Almighty for Who He is - Creator of heaven and earth, Lord of all His creation, Savior of mankind - just to name a few of His eminent positions. And thank Him for His divine attributes — His love, His faith, His power — again just to name a few. You cannot develop a thankful attitude without giving thanks to Yahweh somewhere. The time to start is now.

Again the apostle Paul spurs us on: "In every thing give thanks: for this is the will of God in Christ Jesus concerning you." (I Thessalonians 5:18) If you're not sure what the will of Yahweh is for your life, give thanks. Giving thanks is always His will for your life. Plus when you give thanks, the presence of Yahweh will increase in your life and thus increase your faith for your prayers to be answered. **START PRAYER WITH THANKSGIVING.**

PRAYER PRINCIPLE FOUR

PRAY IN FAITH. I have never heard Elden Shisler ever pray any of the mealy-mouth prayers that I have heard many Christians pray over the years. Elden never prays: "Lord, if it be your will...." When Elden prays, He always prays believing that what He is praying is the Lord's will. Even if he occasionally prays something that is not the Lord's will, Elden still prays it believing that it is the Lord's will. Someone may object that Elden is just wasting his time praying something that is not the Lord's will. I am certain that Elden never consciously prays anything that he knows is not the Master's will. But I am also certain that it is better to pray something that is not the Lord's will in faith, then to pray "Lord, if it be your will..." with little or no faith at all.

In Hebrews we read: "But without faith it is impossible to please him." (Hebrews 11:6) If we can't please Yahweh without faith, then we can't pray to Him successfully without faith. Moreover, if we have no faith, then that's where we need to start — praying that the Almighty will give us faith.

Plus if we lack faith, we need to read the Word of Yahweh because "faith cometh by hearing, and hearing by the word of God." (Romans 10:17)

When Elden Shisler wants the mice out of his room, he sets a few mousetraps and then commands the varmints to leave. That's faith! And the mice disappear. **PRAY IN FAITH**

PRAYER PRINCIPLE FIVE

PRAY UNTIL YOU GET THE ANSWER. When we give up on something that we are praying for, the devil wins. He wins because he gets us to quit before Yahweh answers our prayer. Both the Bible and this book testify to the truth that it is Yahweh's will to answer our prayers. The parable of the unjust judge related in Luke 18:1-8 encourages us to keep praying until Yahweh answers our prayer.

Now someone is probably thinking "I don't want to pray 23 years for Yahweh to answer my prayer." In all likelihood you won't have to pray anywhere near that long. Please notice that the vast majority of Elden's prayers were answered within the first year of when Elden prayed them. Yahweh proclaims over and over in His Word that He answers prayer. However long it takes, **PRAY UNTIL YOU GET THE ANSWER.**

Possibly the reason that Yahweh took over 23 years to answer Elden's persistent prayer to be reunited with his children is so that this book could be written as an encouragement to your faith. Yahweh needs more than Christians who are praying to Him daily; He is looking for prayer warriors who will overcome the devil with their prayers. The devil isn't going to just lay down and let you win without a fight. But if a poorly educated hillbilly from Missouri can rout the devil with his prayers, so can you. The tribulation prophesied in the Bible may be just around the corner. Yahweh

THE PRAYER WARRIOR

is looking for **PRAYER WARRIORS** to make His church victorious in the end.

CHAPTER THIRTY-FIVE

PRAY WITHOUT CEASING

In I Thessalonians 5:17 the apostle Paul admonishes us: "Pray without ceasing." What does this mean? Does it mean that we pray every second of every day? Sometimes we have something important to do that requires our entire focus. How do we pray then when our total focus is on something else? Moreover, if we are to pray every second of every day, how do we pray when we are asleep? Surely "pray without ceasing" does not mean that we are to consciously pray every second of every day. So what does it mean?

Doesn't "pray without ceasing" really mean that our hearts are always to be toward our God no matter what else we are doing? Doesn't this mean that we are to look to Yahweh first before we try to resolve things ourselves? If these thoughts express what "pray without ceasing" really means, then Elden Shisler epitomizes praying without ceasing.

Elden prays every day — many more times than once every day. He has his regular devotional time, but he also prays frequently no matter what else he is doing. Elden quite simply directs his heart toward the Almighty no matter what else he is doing. Moreover, he almost always looks to Yahweh before he tries to resolve things himself. As already stated, he is a living epitome of praying without ceasing.

What makes this all the more amazing is Elden's deficiencies in life. If Elden were growing up today, he probably would have been classified as developmentally disabled. Because of his learning problems, he undoubtedly would have been put in special education. Throw in the health problems of his earlier years and who knows whether anybody in our educational system would have followed up with someone with so many deficiencies as Elden.

Plus Elden has some emotional shortcomings. Sometimes little things really upset him. Sometimes he gets bent out of shape and gets somewhat argumentative. The trauma of Helen leaving him and the years of separation from his children certainly didn't help to calm his already fragile emotions. But whatever his deficiencies in life, Elden had something that always carried him through: he prayed without ceasing! He still prays without ceasing! I have seen people with far greater natural abilities than Elden Shisler give up while handicapped Elden prays through. For every handicapped person reading this book Elden's prayer for you is a simple one: that you would know the Lord as your personal Savior and that you would overcome all your problems through prayer.

In Mark 11:23-24 Yahshua exhorts His disciples: "For verily I say unto you, That whosoever shall say unto this mountain, Be thou removed, and be thou cast into the sea; and shall not doubt in his heart, but shall believe that those things which he saith shall come to pass; he shall have whatsoever he saith. Therefore I say unto you, What things soever ye desire, when ye pray, believe that ye receive them, and ye shall have them." First, Elden was knocking down sand piles with his prayers; then he was tearing down hills. Ultimately he threw a few mountains into the sea with his prayers. To tear down mountains, men use dynamite and bulldozers. Elden's prayers have truly been dynamite in the hands of Yahweh Almighty.

THE PRAYER WARRIOR

Just last week the nozzle for the air hose in our work shed was missing. When Elden discovered it missing, he looked everywhere in the work shed where he thought it might be, but he couldn't find it. So he looked all around outside the work shed, but he still couldn't find it. After going home and eating supper, he came back to the work shed and searched for the air hose nozzle again. As before, no matter where he looked, he could not locate the air hose nozzle. That night before he went to bed, Elden prayed: "Lord, show me where that nozzle is." When he woke up in the morning, he felt Yahshua speak to him, "Steve Dorsey has the nozzle." (Steve Dorsey, although not a church member, rents a small bungalow from New Beginnings Church at Lakeview Hills.) After getting dressed and having his breakfast, Elden went over to Steve's place and knocked on the door. When Steve answered, Elden asked him if he had the nozzle for the air hose. Steve replied that he did, apologized for not returning it right away, and went and got Elden the air hose nozzle. Elden's prayer took care of that sand pile in a flash. Of course, Elden's persistent prayer to find his children moved more than one mountain out of his way. Elden is still praying prayers to throw mountains into the sea. At this writing Elden Shisler is 75 years old, yet his prayer life is as vibrant as ever. His prayers will continue to be answered long after he has left this life.

So I close this book with Elden's prayer for you the reader: "Most Holy loving Heavenly Father, how awesome You are to lead us through the valley of the shadow of death. I pray that this book may be an inspiration to all who read it. Grant all who don't know You the real salvation to make their peace, calling, and election sure. I thank You in the precious name of our Savior Yahshua. Amen and amen!"

ACKNOWLEDGMENTS

The first and primary acknowledgment for this book goes to Yahweh, the Almighty God of heaven and earth. Without His answers to Elden's prayers there never would have been any consideration of writing **"THE PRAYER WARRIOR"**. In fact, hopefully your acknowledgment of Yahweh Almighty increased with your reading this book.

The second acknowledgment goes to Elden Shisler. For the numerous hours that he spent with me in recalling the events of his life I am truly grateful. Also, I want to thank him for his great patience with me in answering my questions and in reviewing episodes in his life that weren't clear to me the first time he related them to me.

All Bible quotations used in **"THE PRAYER WARRIOR"** are taken from the King James version of the Bible. I acknowledge the scholars who took the time to do this enduring Bible translation.

For the events in Elden's life before he moved to Illinois I acknowledge help from all of the following people: David "Ike" Chapman for his confirmation of the events regarding Elden's farm accident in Chapter Nine, the editor of the Milan Standard for allowing me to quote the Milan Standard account of Elden's auto accident related in Chapter Eleven, the nice librarians at the public library in Milan who helped me locate the Milan Standard account of Elden's auto accident, and the medical records clerk at the hospital in Milan who helped me verify the dates of the accidents recorded in Chapters Nine and Eleven.

Special acknowledgments go to Jackie Heino and Judy Smith for their help with the brief accounts of the Sowders Movement and the Dawkins movement related in Chapter Fifteen and to Barry Steinman and Terry Hoffberg for their assistance with the history and details of the Ridott Shop in Chapter Nineteen. Also, a special acknowledgment goes to Terry Witt for his eyewitness account of the splitting of the tornado in Chapter One and his verification of many of the other events in Elden's life. Moreover, a special acknowledgment goes to Mark Vlad for his reading of the rough manuscript and verification of the events in Elden's life from Chapter Fifteen to the end of this book.

Also, I need to thank Elden's daughter Merla Moseley for her critical reading of the rough manuscript and her corrections surrounding the events that involved Elden and her being reunited. In the same vein I thank Elden's daughter Sara Shisler, her good friends Robert and Mary Jane Caples, and again Merla Moseley for their recollections that helped me pin down the events and timing of the momentous phone call recorded in Chapter Twenty-Nine.

Next, special acknowledgment and thanks go to the following people for their reading of the rough manuscript and their suggestions which I incorporated into the manuscript to make this a more readable book: Michael Arndt and my son-in-law Andrew Lodge. Andrew, in particular, helped me weed a lot of stuff out of the manuscript that really wasn't necessary.

Finally, special acknowledgments and thanks go to three people who took the time to read the improved manuscript of **"THE PRAYER WARRIOR"** and provide suggestions which I incorporated into the final text: Susan Brazas, my daughter in-law Kelly Buck, and my nephew John Crocker

Jr. All three of them I thank greatly in helping me to eliminate some unnecessary redundancies from the text.

And last of all, I give credit to Douglas Black for the many hours he spent in formatting **"THE PRAYER WARRIOR"** for me to get the book ready to send to the publisher.